AMERICAN EAGLE CANE STYLE

AMERICAN EAGLE CANE STYLE · TRADITIONAL MARTIAL ARTS

INSTRUCTIONAL TEXTBOOK

Style Founders
Clifford Crandall, Jr., Eric Stalloch, and Lynn Jessee

SECOND EDITION

Published 2019 by
American Martial Arts Institute
Main Office: 8382 Seneca Turnpike
New Hartford, New York 13413
(315) 768-1859
AMAI-EagleStyle.Com

Printed By: Kindle Direct Publishing

Manufactured in the United States of America

ISBN: 9781689224826

Disclaimer:

Although the American Martial Arts Institute, Secure Living Online, and the author of this instructional and informational book (collectively known as AMAI affiliates) have taken great care to ensure the authenticity of the information and techniques contained herein, they are not responsible, in whole or in part, for any injury which may occur to the reader or readers by reading and/ or following the instructions in this publication. They also do not guarantee that the techniques and illustrations described in this will be safe and effective in a self-defense or training situation. It is understood that there exists a potential for injury when using or demonstrating the techniques herein described. It is essential that before following any of the activities, physical or otherwise, herein described, the reader or readers first should consult his or her physician for advice on whether practicing or using the techniques described in this publication could cause injury, physical or otherwise. Since the physical activities described herein could be too sophisticated in nature for the reader or readers, it is essential a physician be consulted. Also, federal, state or local laws may prohibit the use or possession of weapons or tools described herein. A thorough examination must be made of the federal, state and local laws before the reader attempts to use these weapons or tools in a self-defense situation or otherwise. None of the AMAI affiliates guarantee the legality or the appropriateness of techniques or weapons or tools herein contained.

Acknowledgements:

Photographs by Eric Stalloch, Clifford Crandall, Jr. and Lynn Jessee.
Photographs for Cane Types section reprinted with permission of CaneMasters.Com.
Select written segments reprinted from American Eagle Style Instructional Textbook with author's permission.

A Need for the 2nd Edition

There was a time, not so long ago, when only a few instructional martial arts books existed. This was for many reasons: the expense of publication, the limits of technology regarding pictures and charts, a desire for secrecy among some martial artists, and communication challenges between schools teaching the same style; these are but a few of the reasons for so few martial arts books. If a student wanted documentation of what they had been taught, they wrote notes for personal reference and took their own pictures. Personal note-taking still has great value, as do personal pictures and videos.

When the founders of this style chose to write the first edition of this textbook, it was known that a second edition would one day be necessary. The first edition was to share the American Eagle Cane Style with the world, to begin its documented history, and for the instructors and students of this style to be assisted in maintaining consistency in the Art.

Since the first edition, the style's traditional structure has been secured through the recognition and certification of a Headmaster to lead it into the future. The structure of the classes used to present the style has solidified. In addition, there are areas that were not presented in the first edition that are practiced regularly in this style, including kicks and guard hand drills. Finally, a traditional martial art style is much more than the physical skills, it has an emotional depth and awareness. Since the writing of the first edition, the founders have identified a concept central to the style's philosophical direction: Quality of Life. This concept has been shared in this second edition.

Additional growth in the style is also documented outside of this textbook. Look for our instructional video resources as well as supplementary books regarding specifics of this style.

Preface

Within the cover of this book lies more than a style; this book provides a means for you, the reader, and others to improve your quality of life and rekindle your hunger to learn and grow. The book is directed to all men and women and geared to the strongest, most important part of your body, which is your mind. This book is based on the incredible adaptability of the cane. What is a cane - a medical tool, a piece of wood, a piece of metal, adaptive equipment, work of art, a statement, or a label? Truly the cane can be all of these things but it is much more than what we see; rather, it is what we can do mentally, physically and emotionally once we understand it. To a healthy, mobile, and flexible 20-year-old man or woman it is one of the most effective self-defense tools imaginable. To an individual man or woman with a mobility challenge, growing signs of age, or simply the inconveniences of old injuries, it is again one of the most effective self-defense tools imaginable. While at the same time for all of these individuals it is a brain stimulant, a physical workout and a means to develop self-confidence, self-esteem and self-worth. So much is possible from a tool that society has labeled as a crutch.

Because of the passion and love of the cane and all it can do, my co-authors Eric Stalloch and Lynn Jessee and I have poured our combined 118 years of cane knowledge and martial arts training into the American Eagle Cane Style which is presented between the covers of this book. In this style there is much more than the physical movements; there is a mental state of mind which is essential to any traditional martial arts style. The martial arts movements go back hundreds and hundreds of years and with that rich history comes the great gift of tradition. With this wonderful concept of tradition come words such as respect, loyalty, commitment, honor and responsibility. Words that some may feel are being lost in our fast-pace society and shrinking world. But no, they still exist in the traditions of old martial arts and in this style you will find them. May our love for the cane impact you and your love for the cane grow and impact others. In my 55 years of training I would like to say to you as you begin your training: if you question the purpose - train more; if you cannot understand why - train more; if you think you are losing your drive - train more; if you think it is coming too easy - train more; and if you cannot see the answers - train harder. The answers are within you. The style is the tool for you to find them and your effort is the price you must pay.

Clifford C. Crandall Jr.

TABLE OF CONTENTS

Preface

Chapter 4: Stances   61

Chapter 5: Grips   71

Chapter 6: Guard Hand Techniques   79

viii

Chapter 10: Forms 215

Instructional Resources 279

x

CHAPTER 1
INTRODUCTION

INTRODUCTION
ABOUT THE FOUNDERS
HISTORY OF THE STYLE

INTRODUCTION

Words are powerful. They can bring great clarity in bridging the thoughts of one human being with another's or assist one's own mind in better understanding itself. Words are tools of communication, as are sign language, body language, voice inflection, and expression through physical action. Thoughts when put into words can become reality. This instructional textbook presents the American Eagle Cane Style for the world to see, while striving for clarity for its traditions, philosophy, techniques, and concepts.

The challenge is that words have inherent limitations. They can be misunderstood from their intended meaning. They can confine the vastness and openness of a thought or concept to a much narrower idea. This is one of the reasons that a traditional martial art style must be learned in a teacher-student (Master-apprentice) relationship. If asked to picture a cane, what do you see? There are many types, materials, styles, and lengths. After reading this textbook, we hope that your concept of what the cane is and can be will have been expanded. For students of this Art, we hope that your concept of the cane continues to grow and mature through training and time.

Choosing to train in a traditional martial art style, such as the American Eagle Cane Style, can be one of the most challenging and rewarding decisions you can make. As a spectator or new student, it can be difficult to see beyond the superficial etiquettes, terminology, and physical movements to perceive it as something deeper. Yet, for those who choose this Way, their journey can lead them to discover for themselves that which is vital in their own life.

Whether you are a new student, a family member of a student, or someone who is interested in the Cane as a traditional martial art tool, this textbook will help you to better see the American Eagle Cane Style and the school which teaches it. It has been said that the traditional martial arts are 90% mental. While we believe this to be true, for beginner's it is more accurately 90% physical. Through the cane we can train the body to develop better motor coordination and physical skills, and through the body we stimulate the mind. Your own involvement with the cane may mean that you improve balance, strength, and defensive skills. For some students, you will choose it as a Way. Way is an English language translation of the Japanese concept of Do (Tao in Chinese), but here it does not refer to a method of doing something or simply a direction to follow, though this is it, in part. Way can be difficult to express with the limitations of words, but it can more accurately be thought of as a Way of Being in this moment and time. For those who choose it, the American Eagle Cane Style can be a very rewarding Way.

Traditional martial art training is truly self-development. We are all human, and martial artists strive for self-improvement through the development of discipline. We seek to discipline the body and discipline the mind. We seek to excite our emotions and find a balance and harmony with our society and within ourselves. This ambition is never truly achieved, but is constantly sought, and through the process we become stronger for ourselves and our personal commitments to family and community. We seek to move beyond our self-imposed limitations to maximize our potential, and to know where we stand in the world and our daily lives. It has been said that there are no problems, only decisions to be made. American Eagle Cane Style can be a means to engage in this type of self-cultivation.

There are thousands of books regarding the martial arts, but very few document a style. Before the publication of this instructional textbook, students of the American Eagle Cane Style had to rely on their own notes taken after a class or seminar. This textbook has been produced as a means to maintain the high standards of quality and of consistency for the style as it is taught now and as it will be perpetuated through future generations.

The American Eagle Cane Style has been demonstrated around the world and more can be learned at AMAI-EagleStyle.Com

ABOUT THE
HEADMASTER AND FOUNDERS

The Style's First Headmaster: Eric Stalloch

The American Eagle Cane Style was founded by three cane masters, Clifford Crandall Jr., Eric Stalloch, and Lynn Jessee, who desired to maintain hundreds of years' of cane history in a traditional martial arts format. From its inception the three founders oversaw the style's growth and direction. Together they released the 1st edition of the American Eagle Cane Style textbook, documenting 95% of the style for its instructors, future students, and the world to see, but knowing that one day a 2nd edition would need to be released. This was because the traditional structure of the style had not yet been fully secured. While the first edition spoke of a Headmaster, one had yet to be designated.

On June 15, 2019, at a public presentation at the American Martial Arts Institute, Grandmaster Clifford C. Crandall, Jr. and Master Lynn M. Jessee chose the third founder, Master Eric Stalloch to lead the American Eagle Cane Style. Giving him their full support, both Grandmaster Crandall and Master Jessee recognized Eric Stalloch to be the Headmaster and governing voice of the American Eagle Cane Style. They presented him with a signed and sealed certificate designating him as the only 10th Degree Black Belt in this style and the individual who will lead the American Eagle Cane Style into a growing, prosperous future.

This certificate hangs on the wall of the training hall floor alongside the style's "Quality of Life" calligraphy for all to see. Headmaster Stalloch now also bears the responsibility to find, train, designate, and certify a successor to this style who will one day become its second Headmaster when he is gone.

The line of succession for leadership of this style will be found both at the American Martial Arts Institute's main office and training hall and at AMAI-EagleStyle.Com. More about Headmaster Stalloch can be found in the following section about the founders of the style. As discussed in the section of this textbook titled What is the American Eagle Cane Style School?, the American Eagle Cane Style has an "umbrella school" which also houses three other styles. This "umbrella school" is the American Martial Arts Institute and its head and founder is Grandmaster Clifford C. Crandall Jr., and his empty hand martial art style is American Eagle Style. Both Headmaster Stalloch and Master Jessee are also Master Instructors in American Eagle Style, training under Grandmaster Crandall. For the sake of both etiquette and simplicity, each of these individuals will be referred to by their highest rank's title (Grandmaster Crandall, Headmaster Stalloch, and Master Jessee). If you have questions regarding the founders, speak with your instructor for clarification and visit AMAI-EagleStyle.com for the most current information regarding these individuals.

Headmaster Certification

The American Eagle Cane Style was founded by three cane masters who desired to maintain hundreds of years' of cane history in a traditional martial arts format. This has been accomplished over the past years, leaving only one last act to secure this style on its traditional road into the future: the completion of the pyramid. In other words, there can only be one at the top.

True leadership does not happen because you want it, but rather because the participants want you.

In this traditional fashion two of the three founders, Grandmaster Clifford C. Crandall Jr. and Master Lynn M. Jessee, have chosen the third founder, Master Eric Stalloch, to lead this style. Giving him their full support, both Grandmaster Clifford Crandall Jr. and Master Lynn Jessee recognize

Eric J. Stalloch

to be the Headmaster and governing voice of the American Eagle Cane Style. He is recognized by these two individuals as the only 10th degree in this style and the individual who will lead the American Eagle Cane Style into a growing, prosperous future.

Signed and certified this day, June 15, 2019.

Clifford C. Crandall, Jr.
Founder

Lynn M. Jessee
Founder

About the Founders
Clifford Crandall, Jr., Eric Stalloch, and Lynn Jessee

Martial art styles are diverse with a vast history stretching back hundreds of years and spanning the globe. For those compelled to better understand the various Arts, it is necessary to look beyond the physical techniques and forms and study the time period, geography, culture, language, and masters who founded each particular Tradition. The founders of traditional martial art styles were first students who trained under other masters, in other styles, before being recognized as the originator of their own particular Art. Their lineage may be traced back in time through credible instructors and established traditions that perpetuate a consistent philosophy, methods, and techniques that have been strictly administrated through a school.

The American Eagle Cane Style was founded by Grandmaster Clifford Crandall, Jr., Headmaster Eric Stalloch, and Master Lynn Jessee based on their combined 118 years of cane knowledge. Headmaster Stalloch and Master Jessee began their training as students of Grandmaster Crandall in the 1980s, with the core of their traditional martial arts foundation stemming from his empty-hand American Eagle Style and the American Martial Arts Institute. Therefore, the American Eagle Cane Style has a history based on more than 50 years from when Grandmaster Crandall first began training and a deeper heritage into what we sometimes refer to as "the old ways" through the lineage of those teachers who instructed him.

In the American Eagle Cane Style, Headmaster Stalloch holds the rank of 10th Degree Black Belt and Grandmaster Clifford Crandall, Jr and Master Lynn Jessee each hold the rank of 9th Degree Black Belt. As founders of this traditional style, they have collaborated on numerous books, DVDs, seminars, programs, classes, public service announcements, articles, television programs, performances, and more around the world for several decades. Below you will find more information about each founder's professional and educational backgrounds and their martial arts experience. These are not complete biographies, but are intended to give you a better understanding on what led to this instructional textbook and style.

Grandmaster Clifford Crandall, Jr.

Grandmaster Crandall began formally training in the martial arts in1966 in Iowa while he was a student pursuing a degree in criminal justice. At that time he was training in the Arts of Judo and Jujutsu.

Loyalty is crucial to the traditional martial arts practitioner; it is the bedrock of the student-instructor relationship and one that Grandmaster Crandall, Headmaster Stalloch, and Master Jessee value as essential.

Grandmaster Crandall's training has taken him around the world and afforded him the opportunity to train under or with many truly knowledgeable and skilled martial artists; however, this was all made possible by following a single path, by staying consistent and true to a foundation. He did not jump from instructor to instructor, rather followed a single traditional Way that provided the opportunity to learn and experience more. Therefore, when he returned to New York State, he joined the Moo Do Kwan under Grandmaster Park Chul Hee, starting over as a white belt. Moo Do Kwan later came to be known as the Kang Duk Won Mudo Association and eventually became the American Kang Duk Won Association. This traditional Tae Kwon Do style was to form the core of Grandmaster Crandall's training. Hanging on the wall of our main training hall is a certificate designating Grandmaster Crandall as a Master Instructor in American Kang Duk Won. This certificate is signed by the late Grandmaster Raymond P. Arndt (1934-2010), who was the head of that school and style.

Grandmaster Arndt enlisted in the United States Army in 1954 and was stationed in Okinawa and later South Korea, giving him years of training in traditional Okinawan Goju Ryu and Korean Tae Kwan Do. While stationed in Seoul,

Korea, he met and befriended Master Kum Chun Kim, an unusually gifted martial artist who served as a chief instructor for Kang Duk Won under Park Chul Hee. Masters Arndt and Kim trained rigorously together. During this time period, and because of Grandmaster Arndt's success and skilled students, Master Park named him as the East Coast Representative of the Kang Duk Won organization in the United States.

It was during this time that Grandmaster Crandall trained under Grandmaster Park Chul Hee and Master Kum Chun Kim. Under Master Kim, Grandmaster Crandall earned the rank of fourth degree black belt. Upon Master Kim's passing in 1983, Master Arndt became the Grandmaster of the American Kang Duk Won Association. Grandmaster Crandall continued his training under Grandmaster Arndt, eventually earning the rank of sixth dan and later Master Instructor. He served as the Executive Director of the American Kang Duk Won Association from 1988 until 1995 before eventually forming his own style, American Eagle Style, and opening the American Martial Arts Institute. What had become a close friendship and sharing of knowledge continued between Grandmaster Crandall and Grandmaster Arndt until Grandmaster Arndt's passing in 2010.

In 1996, Clifford Crandall, Jr. was promoted and bestowed the title of Grandmaster (10th Dan) by the Grandmaster of the Tong Leong Gwo Shuh Goan International Organization, Headmaster Manuel Agrella, who represented the Soke Council of Grandmasters on the East Coast. This recognized Grandmaster Crandall as the Grandmaster for the American Eagle Style and American Martial Arts Institute.

There are two credible paths to holding the title of Grandmaster or Headmaster. The first is by succession. An individual is designated as the heir to a style by the previous Grandmaster, and the position is bestowed upon the previous Grandmaster's death. This creates an unbroken lineage of Grandmasters who perpetuate the style as a living structure, unchanged from one generation to the next. The second method is for a credible individual, one who is a master in an established style, to formulate their own style and to be recognized by the Grandmaster of another style.

Grandmaster Crandall has trained in three Japanese styles. In 1984, he traveled to Japan and trained under Master Sekichi Toguchi, who was the head of Okinawan Goju-ryu. This was done with support from Grandmaster Raymond P. Arndt. Grandmaster Crandall is also the Headmaster of the Iaido (sword) style Takenouchi-Hangan-Ryu-Matsuno-Crandall. His certified position and title were bestowed by his instructor, Headmaster Tsuneyoshi Matsuno during a traditional ceremony in Kobe, Japan in June 2002. The ceremony was filmed and a documentary was released and aired on television in Central New York called "The Passing of the Sword." Grandmaster Crandall began training under Tsuneyoshi Matsuno in 1985 after having him as a guest on his television program, the *Martial Arts Today Show*. The passing of Headmaster Matsuno in February of 2005 made Grandmaster Crandall the head of this 300-year old traditional samurai iaido style for the world. Headmaster Matsuno had directed Grandmaster Crandall to add his name to the style, making it Takenouchi-Hangan-Ryu-Matsuno-Crandall, telling him that he would add to the style's future.

In 2006, a year after Headmaster Matsuno's unexpected passing, Grandmaster Crandall's longtime martial arts friend, Master Fumio Demura, wrote him a letter offering the opportunity to become his student in the Art of Batto-do. He accepted this invitation and is now one of Master Demura's students. In 2006, this batto organization was known as the Society for the Preservation of Toyama-Ryu Batto-do, but in 2016 Master Demura renamed his batto Art as Suishin-Ryu meaning the "Water Mind School" (or Tradition). Grandmaster Crandall fulfilled late Headmaster Tsuneyoshi Matsuno's wishes for the future development of Takenouchi-Hangan-Ryu-Matsuno-Crandall by incorporating Master Demura's batto-do teachings into the style. He documented this art in the textbook and a 2-disc instructional DVD set called Takenouchi-Hangan-Ryu-Matsuno-Crandall Iaido Style and Batto-Do.

Prior to becoming a full-time, professional martial artist, Grandmaster Crandall was a New York State certified classroom teacher, elementary school principal, high school principal, and superintendent of schools. He left the public education profession in 1984 to dedicate himself to the martial arts full-time. This allowed him to travel to 22 different countries and train with martial artists around the world. It was during this time, through producing and hosting the Martial Arts Today television program, that he had the opportunity to train in China under Xiang Li Li in Tai Chi Chuan.

While Grandmaster Crandall has trained with knowledgeable and skilled martial artists from around the world, the individuals mentioned above are the primary instructors under who he has trained. Copies of his certifications may be found on public display at all full-time locations of the American Martial Arts Institute.

Grandmaster Crandall has made numerous contributions to the martial arts around the world and in community safety programs. In 2008, he co-founded Secure Living Online, with his long-time student, Headmaster Eric Stalloch, with Master Lynn Jessee and American Eagle Style Master Cheryl Freleigh, serving on the board of directors. This agency provides seminars, consultation, and instructional media for health, awareness, and personal safety for people of all ages and abilities. More can be learned at SecureLivingOnline.Com. Together with Headmaster Stalloch and Master Jessee, he has taught seminars for the Central Association for the Blind and Visually Impaired, Hunter College graduate students, Active Seniors and more. Their seminar for Active Seniors was featured on a segment of the TodayShow.Com. Grandmaster Crandall presented to surgeons, administrators, and physical therapists at Jacksonville Hospital in Florida regarding how the cane benefits stroke and heart attack survivor's recovery. He also co-authored the book Moving Beyond Disabilities with Linda Möller. A full list of his publications is available at AMAI-EagleStyle.Com.

In 2000, Grandmaster Crandall made it possible for two of his American Eagle Style black belt instructors to train as students of the Cane Masters System. They were Eric Stalloch and Lynn Jessee. This began years of training in the Cane under the supervision and direction of Grandmaster Crandall. In 2007, they earned the rank of First Dan and later Canemaster in the Cane Master System, alongside Grandmaster Crandall. In 2016, Grandmaster Shuey promoted Grandmaster Crandall and Master Jessee to 8th degree within his organization and Headmaster Stalloch to 9th degree, identifying him as the successor to his style and programs for the world. More can be learned about their involvement with Cane Masters in the History section of this textbook.

Headmaster Eric Stalloch

Headmaster Stalloch is the 10th Degree Black Belt for the American Eagle Cane Style, an 8th Degree Black Belt in American Eagle Style, and has been a student of Grandmaster Clifford Crandall, Jr. since 1989. In August 2013, he was certified by Grandmaster Crandall as the Master of American Eagle Style and as his successor to the title of Grandmaster for the American Martial Arts Institute and American Eagle Style.

Headmaster Stalloch also has an extensive educational background, centered on his Permanent New York State Teaching Certification with over 20 years of experience teaching biology to grades 10-12. He has a Master's Degree from Syracuse University in Science Education.

Headmaster Stalloch is the proprietor of a full-time training hall for the American Martial Arts Institute. He is also an advanced student in Takenouchi-Hangan-Ryu-Matsuno-Crandall Iaido. Together with Grandmaster Crandall, Headmaster Stalloch co-founded Secure

Living Online, which presents health, awareness, and personal safety seminars for people of all ages and capabilities. Secure Living Online seminars have been featured in international media including MSNBC's TodayShow.com and *Combat Magazine*. With Grandmaster Crandall, he has taught seminars for individuals who are blind or visually impaired, children, teenagers, adult men and women, active seniors, and people with mobility challenges.

Headmaster Stalloch has partnered with Grandmaster Crandall to write and produce Secure Living Public Service Announcements which air across Central New York State and internationally online. Together Headmaster Stalloch and Grandmaster Crandall have collaborated to remind people of all ages how to be safer in a constantly changing world. Their combined efforts have had a positive impact on community safety.

Headmaster Stalloch has represented the American Martial Arts Institute internationally, performing and competing in the kata and sparring divisions of the Russian International Tournament in 1997 in St. Petersburg. He also shared his enthusiasm for the arts when teaching katas in Australia during the American-Australian Martial Arts Exchange in 2005. He has also represented the school in Japan, Italy, and the Caribbean.

In addition to co-authoring *Be Safe Physically and Mentally with the Crandall System* and *Leadership Piece by Piece*, he has produced 10 instructional DVDs with Grandmaster Crandall including *Practical Cane Self-Defense*, Cane-*Fu: Moving Beyond Disabilities*, and the *American Cane System DVD series* Levels 1-8. He has written articles for *Taekwondo Times*, *Inside Kung Fu*, *Combat*, *Action Martial Arts Magazine*, and others. Some of these articles include exclusive interviews with martial artists including Shihan Fumio Demura, Headmaster Tsuneyoshi Matsuno, Master Frank Dux, Grandmaster Mark Shuey, Sr., Master Alan Goldberg, and others.

With Grandmaster Crandall's support, in 2000 he began years of training with the cane through the Cane Master program affiliated with Grandmaster Mark Shuey, eventually being promoted to the rank of 9th Dan and the position of successor within that organization. Today, he continues to support the Cane Masters organization, overseeing its East Coast Help Center for Grandmaster Shuey. In support of Grandmaster Shuey's virtual dojo, he collaborated with Grandmaster Crandall and Master Jessee to write the *American Cane System Guidebook*.

Master Lynn Jessee

Master Lynn Jessee started training in the martial arts in 1982. Over the decades she has sought to share her passion for the martial arts and how it may improve people's lives and strengthen our communities. In the 80's and 90's she taught seminars and programs such as "Say No to Drugs" and "Reading Advocacy and the Martial Arts" for the public school system students K-12, participated in lectures and demonstrations about the martial arts for the Ontario County Public Library System, and taught Women's Self Defense classes as well as Tot-Awareness seminars for ages 3-5.

As a member of the Board of Directors of Secure Living Online, she continues to be involved in teaching a wide variety of populations, such as seniors, people with disabilities or visual impairments, women, and children, about safety, awareness, and wellness.

From 1995 to 1997 Master Jessee served as a Senior Instructor in the American Martial Arts Institute, acting as the supervising administrator for one of the fulltime locations. She is a certified Master Instructor in the American Eagle Style under the direction of Grandmaster Crandall, holding the rank of 7th degree black belt, and has served as a chief judge in numerous national and international tournaments. She represented American martial artists from this traditional school as a member of the American-Japanese Goodwill Tour in 2002, and the American Martial Arts Institute Caribbean Training Cruise in 2013.

With Grandmaster Crandall's support, in 2000 she began years of training with the cane through the Cane Master program affiliated with Grandmaster Mark Shuey, eventually being promoted to the rank of 8th Dan and the position of Senior Canemaster within that organization.

Master Jessee co-produced 10 instructional DVDs with Masters Stalloch and Crandall, including the eight instructional DVDs for the American Cane System, *Cane-Fu: Moving Beyond Disabilities*, and *Practical Cane Self-Defense Volume 1*. She was a collaborator on *Just Get Away*, an informational guide for Secure Living Online used in seminars for people of all ages and abilities. She was also a collaborating author on the *American Cane System Guidebook* for the Cane Masters International Association. In 2019, she co-authored *Women's Self Defense in a Changing World* with Grandmaster Crandall.

Alongside Headmaster Stalloch, she assisted in the teaching of cane seminars at the Action Martial Arts Hall of Honors in Atlantic City, New Jersey.

In addition, Master Jessee's educational background includes an M.S. in Biology from the University of Rochester and an Associate of Science as a Physical Therapist Assistant from Hesser College. She is currently a Licensed Physical Therapist Assistant in the State of New Hampshire, but has also worked as a Senior Technical Associate for a research lab, as a supervisor for a clinical lab, and in other biological professional settings. She has published numerous papers in the field. She is also a Certified Personal Trainer through the American College of Sports Medicine. Her unique background gives her insight to body mechanics and how they change with age.

The combination of the three founders' professional and educational backgrounds makes the founding of the American Eagle Cane Style truly unique.

American Eagle Cane Style

Today Headmaster Stalloch sets the direction for this style with support from the other founding Masters. Together they continue to teach and train a staff of adult black belt instructors and instructors' assistants, which Headmaster Stalloch certifies annually to teach the style, maintaining its consistency, standards, philosophy, and educational structure. They share their love of the Art, knowledge, and skills with all students of this style by continuing to teach classes. You will learn more about this style in the pages that come. It is now for the style to stand the test of time.

HISTORY OF THE CANE

The cane has been used and documented in some of the earliest written records, such as the biblical story of Moses and his walking cane staff. This non-offensive, seemingly unimportant item is almost invisible in the world as it is taken for granted by most people on a daily basis. Because of this mental image held by so many, the cane has been used historically as a method of concealing swords, knives, poison darts (with the cane as the blow gun), poison powders, money, drugs, important papers, as a number of customized rifles and pistols, as break apart nunchaku, and as a hiding place for manriki or a pop-up umbrella. It has been featured in James Bond movies, Miracle on 34th Street, and it has shown its versatility in recent movies such as the Kingsmen. So much potential, yet, by itself with no modifications, a simple wooden cane is one of the most successful and immediately available self-defense tools today.

The cane's history as it applies to the American Eagle Cane Style goes back to some of the earliest martial arts documentations of tools used for defense. Here it shares a similarity with traditional Okinawan and Japanese kubudo weapons such as the bo, sai, nunchaku, tonfa, and kama, which originated as agricultural tools but were later adapted as weapons of defense. Just as these tools became parts of empty hand martial art styles or as distinct weapons systems, the cane became a versatile weapon in China, Japan, Korea, Egypt, India, the Philippines, England, France, the United States, and other countries. Records from scrolls, murals, carvings, and other sources clearly indicate that the cane was being used as a martial weapon for hundreds of years.

The cane (ji pang ee) has had a long tradition in Korean martial arts styles. Earliest records suggest it was popularized by Buddhist monks, including Won Gwang who was enlisted by King Jinpyeong (the 24th ruler of the Silla Kingdom) to teach the Hwa Rang warriors. In fact, the cane was used by at least three ancient Korean martial systems: the Sado Mu Sool (tribal family martial art), the Bulkyo Mu Sool (Buddhist martial art), and the Koong Joong Mu Sool (royal court martial art). Notably, the Buddhist monks focused on defensive techniques of submission and evasion unless defending their country; whereas, the royal court exclusively used offensive techniques to protect the court. They also incorporated canes with hidden blades and poisons. In relatively modern times, Hapkido has utilized the cane since its inception.

Japan's use of the cane is equally ancient. It is commonly referred to as tsune, tsue, tanjo, and hanbo (each varies slightly in length and design). The art of Sutekki-jutsu, founded by Uchida Ryogoro (1837-1921), and now called tanjo-jutsu, used a Western-style walking cane as a martial weapon as a means to popularize the traditional Japanese style of Jodo (a short staff). *Kenbu*, published in 1898, details a shikomi tsue (sword hidden in cane) kata. Ryukyu Ode Hiden Bujutsu (the secret royal martial arts of Ryukyu), developed around 1600, also included the study of the cane. Ryukyu is an archipelago, including Okinawa, which was occupied by Japan at the time. It is well-known that bladed weapons were banned by decree by the occupying government which led to the development of alternative defense methods.

Canes have also been a status symbol in numerous countries. In 1937, the New York Times published an article titled "Tokyo Ruler Honors Aides with Right to Carry Canes." Similarly, in the United States, President Theodore Roosevelt presented canes from historic woods for members of his cabinet, and George Washington received one of Benjamin Franklin's canes as a sign of admiration. Canes were even used as status symbols by the Pharaohs of ancient Egypt, with King Tutankhamen being entombed with 132 walking sticks.

It is well documented that monks of ancient China utilized canes. This is often referred to as the Shaolin cane, Dharma cane, Zhang, and by others terms. It is used in forms of taichi and wushu. Cane techniques can also be implemented with an umbrella; in fact, there are entire traditional umbrella forms. "Umbrella of Dragon and Tiger" is a 69-move form of Hung Ka Pugilism and was documented by Master Ho Lap Tin.

In 1898, an Englishman, Edward William Barton-Wright, invented a self-defense system utilizing the cane called Bartitsu. Born in India, Barton-Wright lived in Japan for many years before returning to England to live. While in Japan he trained in jujutsu, which he used as the foundation for his cane self-defense art. He brought two jujutsu masters to England to teach at his studio, and Sir Arthur Conan Doyle even referenced Sherlock Holmes's using Baritsu [sic].

In France, La Canne, is a traditional system of French stick fighting developed by Pierre Vigny, who trained in Savate. He published "Self Defense with a Walking Stick" in 1902 in Pearson's Magazine. In 1923, in India, an officer of the Indian Police published "The Walking Stick Method of Self-Defense" based on Vigny's system. This later became the basis for self-defense training for tens of thousands living in Palestine in the 1940s.

Despite the cane's long history, it became socially stigmatized as a device for persons with mobility challenges or advanced age. Even among martial artists it was considered a relatively obscure weapon with few practitioners or modern systems dedicated to its use. In late 1990's, Grandmaster Mark Shuey, founder of the American Cane System, envisioned the cane as a mainstream self-defense tool for modern times, one to be taught by martial art schools around the world, and one to be used by the general public, especial senior citizens.

As the founder of the Cane Masters International Association, he began to handcraft quality canes for self-defense and exercise that were also aesthetically beautiful. At the time, the few canes being used by martial artists were basic metal collapsible canes or rattan varieties. Grandmaster Shuey made his canes out of oak and hickory, developing features such as hand grips, specialty crooks, and numerous other features. The creation of a cane which could withstand the demands of traditional martial arts training has been credited as a critical advancement in modern times. He taught hundreds of seminars around the world, and released the Cane Master program through a series of DVDs.

In 2010, a series of eight instructional DVDs were released, the *American Cane System Ranking Series*, which served as a reference material for eight gyups. In 2016, he certified Cane Master Instructor Eric Stalloch as his successor, ensuring continuity of leadership for his programs.

American Eagle Cane Style

In 2000, Cane Master Clifford Crandall, Jr., as Grandmaster of the American Martial Arts Institute, made it possible for two of his American Eagle Style black belt instructors to train as students of the Cane Masters System. They were Eric Stalloch and Lynn Jessee. This began years of training in the Cane under the supervision and direction of Grandmaster Crandall. In 2007, they earned the rank of First Dan and later Canemaster in the Cane Master System, alongside Master Crandall.

Master Crandall's personal awareness and use of the cane dated back to the early 1980s. In 1983, he traveled to Japan to live and train in Okinawan Goju Ryu under the late Headmaster Sekichi Toguchi. While there, Headmaster Toguchi and Grandmaster Crandall became friends in the martial arts and exchanged philosophies and traditions. One of Headmaster Toguchi's favorite katas was his cane kata. On a day of celebration and socializing Grandmaster Crandall performed his favorite tonfa kata for Headmaster Toguchi and his brown and black belts. After his presentation Headmaster Toguchi went out on the training floor and had it explained in English to Grandmaster Crandall that this was his favorite weapons kata. With that he performed a powerful and complex cane kata. This changed how Grandmaster Crandall thought of the cane and is one of the reasons it is an extension tool in his empty hand style.

In 1994, Master Crandall demonstrated the cane self defense techniques as the leader of the China America Team, the first American martial artists to perform in the People's Republic of China by government invitation. In addition, Master Crandall traveled the world as the host of the Martial Arts Today Show, covering martial arts in 22 countries including Japan, China, France, Belize, Guatemala, Russia, Hong Kong, and many others.

In 2007, with three certified Canemasters, the American Martial Arts Institute became the East Coast Help Center for the Cane Masters International Association, to support Grandmaster Crandall's longtime friend, Mark Shuey. Cane classes were offered to the public, seminars and public demonstrations were organized and taught, and Masters Crandall, Stalloch, and Jessee began to further develop their cane programs. These included personal safety for individuals who were Blind and Visually Impaired (for the Central Association for the Blind and Visually Impaired), for people with mobility challenges (through the production of the one-hour DVD *Cane-Fu: Moving Beyond Disabilities*), for Active Seniors (with their seminar featured on the Today Show.Com), and many others. In 2011, Masters Crandall, Stalloch, and Jessee were the first martial artists ever invited to present at the New York State Association for Education and Rehabilitation of the Blind and Visually Impaired, teaching to professionals and clients on cane techniques.

Articles were written by Masters Crandall, Stalloch, and Jessee, many featuring the techniques they had developed. These articles were published by *Inside Kung Fu*, *Combat* (in the UK), *Action Martial Arts Magazine*, and others. Masters Jessee and Stalloch assisted in teaching seminars at the Action Martial Arts Hall of Honors in Atlantic City for martial artists from hundreds of schools around the world. In 2005, Master Stalloch demonstrated and taught the cane in Australia for martial artists from 150 different martial arts schools around the country as part of the America-Australia Goodwill Tour team.

Masters Crandall, Stalloch, and Jessee wished to share some of their techniques and katas with the world, resulting in the one-hour instructional DVD *Practical Cane Self-Defense, Volume 1*, which included numerous cane techniques and the form Natural Walk, a kata that had been designed by Masters Crandall and Stalloch. Additionally, at the same time, Master Jessee designed Autumn Wind.

Grandmaster Shuey recognized their educational presentation skills, and in 2008, asked them to assist him with the structuring of the Cane Master's system into a new organized system, one with eight colored belt ranks and 10 degrees of black belt. Masters Crandall, Stalloch, and Jessee accepted this responsibility, developing five new katas, Reflection 1-5. After two years of planning and preparation, they filmed, edited, and released internationally the eight instructional DVDs: *American Cane System Ranking Series*. These became a resource for the Cane Masters organization and supported Grandmaster Shuey's programs including Cane-Fu, Cane-Chi, Silver Dragons, Cane-Ja, Yoga Play, and others.

In 2017, Grandmaster Shuey decided that to reach the world's population with the benefits of the cane he would have to make a true leap of faith. His desire was always to reach as many people as possible with no limitation on their involvement with the cane, and give them the skills and direction to pass his knowledge on to others. His love of the traditions was still important, but his desire to help everyone was stronger. As a result he recognized the writings and skill levels as well as the traditionalism that was the foundation of the work of Master Stalloch, Master Jessee and Master Crandall. His hope was that the cane could still have roots in the martial arts traditions through their future efforts. He promoted Master Crandall and Master Jessee to 8th degree within his organization and Master Stalloch to 9th degree, identifying him as the successor to his style and programs for the world. In 2017, Grandmaster Shuey's American Cane System linked with the world through his Virtual Dojo at CaneMastersDojo.Com. The Facebook link to this Dojo exploded; within three weeks he had over 4,500 followers and his leap of faith was beginning to be realized.

At the same time his three highest ranking instructors made their commitment to safeguard the traditions of the martial arts and of the cane for the few that would walk the structured path of traditional martial arts. Still an active part of the American Cane System under Grandmaster Shuey, Master Stalloch, Master Jessee and Master Crandall documented their collective 118 years of cane knowledge into a traditional style called the American Eagle Cane Style. On September 10, 2017 Grandmaster Shuey, along with Master Crandall and Master Stalloch, announced via live feed on his Virtual American Cane System site the American Eagle Cane Style and its three founders. As part of this airing Master Crandall and Master Stalloch presented two cane techniques from Grandmaster Shuey's system. They also reminded the viewers that although they teach a traditional format and different style than Grandmaster Shuey, that their school (the American Martial Arts Institute) is still the Instructional Help Center for the East Coast, providing assistance to those who wish to achieve rank or certification under Grandmaster Shuey's programs. This was shared on social media and posted on the Internet.

The old way is not necessarily the right way or the only way, but must be kept alive as a choice for those who seek it. The American Eagle Cane Style recognizes the benefits of the internet, books, videos, Facebook and other social media. However, the American Eagle Cane Style holds to the belief that traditional instruction is perpetuated through the personal growth of a student apprenticing under a Master in person; and that loyalty, respect, etiquette and accountability are as essential to a good style as a kick, punch, parry or block. As you seek the history of the three founders of this style you will see that their training and years of commitment radiate with these concepts and as a result have benefited them throughout their lives.

Learn more about its continuing history at AmericanEagleCaneSystem.Com or AMAI-EagleStyle.com.

CHAPTER 2
SCHOOL AND STYLE

PHILOSOPHY
SCHOOL OF AMERICAN EAGLE CANE STYLE
ETIQUETTE
SCHOOL BACKGROUND
INSTRUCTOR STATUS

Philosophy

Traditional martial arts have a structure that tests our resolve and increases our feelings of responsibility to others. When we talk of the philosophy of a style, we are referring to the basic nature of the style and how it applies to the student and how they view their surroundings.

The American Eagle Cane Style identifies the cane as adaptive equipment that will allow the user to lead a better, more complete and active life. This style guides the student to understand that they are important and have a great deal to offer to their families, friends, and community. Through training, the cane becomes an extension of your body and therefore an extension of you. As you train with the cane it shapes you into a more physically and mentally responsive and active individual. Through training you see a better life for yourself and in turn wish to use your energy to help those around you have a better life. This concept, which is the philosophy of the style, will grow as you walk the road of traditional training in the American Eagle Cane Style.

Quality of Life

Each day brings new challenges and decisions to be made. The journey of an American Eagle Cane Stylist is to a destination that has not changed among Traditionalist in hundreds of years. The compass always points North, and we are drawn in this direction. But as we travel this Way, what is it that we are seeking? The physical skills of self-defense, improvement of balance, and expression through body movement are easily seen and identified. Philosophy and underlying purpose of the Art are always in practice, but we can lose sight of them in the many changes life brings. To help remind American Eagle Cane Stylists why we train and what we seek, the founders have identified a core concept. Put to paper with ink and brush by Grandmaster Clifford Crandall, a calligraphy hangs on the wall in our main training hall. This calligraphy states what we seek, which is "Quality of Life." We believe that you can find quality of life in each day by training. Through your mental state and choice, each day is lived to its fullest potential. We choose to deny that which can diminish us because we care about ourselves and others. We recognized that we have a great deal to offer our family, friends, and community. For those of you who have chosen the American Eagle Cane Style as a Way, we hope you never stop seeking Quality of Life.

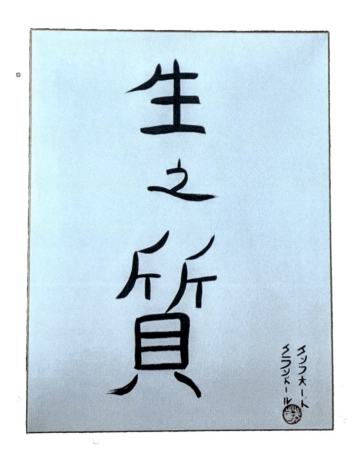

What is the
American Eagle Cane Style School?

If you consider a style, such as the American Eagle Cane Style, as a fluid you can compare it to a gallon of water. Then the school, in this case the American Martial Arts Institute, would be the container the water is kept in. The style as water has properties that cannot be altered without losing the essence of what it is. For example if we heat water to its boiling point we get steam and in turn lose the ability to quench our thirst with it. So there are properties such as rules and regulations within the style. Yet the free-flow of the style and its importance to quench our thirst for knowledge and skills is not so specific as to establish how it is shared or maintained. The school or container does that. The container allows you only to get water from the nearest opening and in an order as it is poured. For example, a white belt may want the green belt kata but the structure of the school makes it so you can only receive the white belt kata and in time the yellow belt kata before you can get to the green belt kata. The knowledge of the style is shared with those who have proven themselves ready. Should a yellow belt receive techniques that could easily be misused or could result in hurting the student themselves? No, they should not receive what they are unready to understand or appreciate. No more than a 5-year-old is presented with a loaded gun as a birthday gift. The 5-year-old may grow up to enjoy skeet shooting with friends or hunting with his family but those opportunities will come later. At five years of age it is more important they develop respect, listening to others who are more experienced, and learning skills of general safety for themselves and others first.

The American Eagle Cane Style has a school or umbrella structure referred to as the American Eagle Cane System. It is seldom looked at because the American Martial Arts Institute maintains the shape of the container for the four styles under its umbrella. If a class was to be started for the American Eagle Cane Style someplace away from the American Martial Arts Institute, you would then see the American Eagle Cane System's umbrella. This container is designed like the American Martial Arts Institute and determines who can sign up, what qualifications they must have to train in this cane style, and the uniform, ranking, age requirement, fees charged and testing structures. All of these areas assist to keep the style, locations, and availability consistent for its students. Without this school structure the style, like a gallon of water, would lay on the floor with everyone trying to get some as it becomes dirty and lost in the corners or through the cracks in the floor. The school keeps order and allows you to know within reason who you will be training next to.

The following are structures of the container which holds the water we all wish to drink called "American Eagle Cane Style." May your thirst never be fully quenched and you learn to share what knowledge you have gained with others appropriately.

Etiquette

The American Eagle Cane Style is a style with the traditional etiquettes of the earliest martial arts styles. As in the traditional Japanese Tea Ceremony it is not the drinking of the tea that is important; it is the method by how you approach the drinking, the company you are in, and the tea room's Zengo which stimulates thought. In this traditional cane style the etiquette can look very much like old tradition military behavior. On the surface the chumbis, meditation posture, bowing, and use of "Sir" and "Ma'am," along with a clean, pressed uniform and a positive attitude look very military. These are the outward signs of something different than just discipline and training. These are some of the signs that reflect the individual's appreciation for the knowledge given, respect for the teacher sharing this knowledge, loyalty for that teacher, and pride in your style and school. Physical movements and gestures of etiquette arise from the growing emotional state of the student, which enables them to become an integral part of the style and school. In effect, the school and its members are becoming a second home and second family to the student in his or her life.

Therefore, bowing and how you bow as seen by others does make a difference. So does the cleanliness of your uniform, hands and face. How you approach an instructor and walk away from them. Also your use of language and behavior in and around the training hall. The higher the rank of a student, the more they are available to assist an instructor in preparing for class, or as a tool to demonstrate as needed to teach lower ranks. Good posture, a positive attitude to help the instructor, and an eagerness to help the school grow and share its knowledge with others are demonstrated by good etiquette.

Clifford P. Crandall Jr.

SCHOOL GUIDELINES AND BACKGROUND

Uniforms, Patches, and Belts

Uniforms fulfill several purposes for a traditional school. They allow the practitioner freedom of motion in the joints and muscles while covering exposed skin for safer training. They visually identify positions of rank or responsibility within the school, allowing students, instructors, and others to know something about the individual's status within the organization. They also establish a clean, professional atmosphere; one which puts the student into a particular frame of mind for training the whole self while conforming to the school's standards. They are also a source of pride and camaraderie for the school. With all of this in mind, the following is information regarding uniforms.

Students

Students wear white pants, a white uniform top, and a white t-shirt (no writing or images) under the white uniform top. The American Eagle Cane Style logo patch is worn on the right lapel.

Instructors' Assistant

Instructors' Assistants wear white pants, a white uniform top with black trim, and a black t-shirt (no writing or images) under the uniform top. The American Eagle Cane Style logo patch is worn on the right lapel.

Instructor

Instructors wear white pants, a black uniform top, and a black t-shirt (no writing or images) under the uniform top. The American Eagle Cane Style logo patch is worn on the right lapel. If an American Eagle Cane Style instructor is also a certified American Eagle Style instructor for the American Martial Arts Institute, they will also wear the American Eagle Style logo patch on their left lapel, allowing them to wear the same uniform top for both styles.

Master Instructor

Master Instructors wear the same uniforms as an instructor. In addition a patch is worn on the right sleeve indicating that they are a Master Instructor. The status of Master is earned at the rank of 6th degree black belt, and "Master" is added to this student's name when they are addressed.

Founders / Successor

The founders of the style wear the Master Instructor uniform and patches. In addition, they wear embroidered belts with the style name and their last name. The style's designated successor will also wear the embroidered belt.

Headmaster

The Headmaster wears the same uniform as an instructor but their belt has their title, name, style name, and school embroidered in blue.

Titled Instructors

A titled instructor is an administrative position. This is not a rank and these positions can be added or removed to meet the needs of the school. The titles are Senior Instructor and Chief Instructor. Titles are identified by wearing a patch on the right upper sleeve.

Black Pants and the American Martial Arts Institute

The American Martial Arts Institute is a school that umbrella's three traditional styles, all with the same rich heritage of philosophy and code of ethics. The values, ethics, morality, and direction of a style is set by the founder or Grandmaster. This school direction permeates the style and its teachings. It comes from the teachings of the Grandmaster's instructors, and the Grandmaster's many years of training, learning, and experiences. In effect is the core of the Grandmaster or Headmaster's approach to the art, their instructors, students and community. This visual but yet invisible thread emanates from the Grandmaster who is identified in the American Martial Arts Institute as the only individual who wears black pants.

BELTS and RANKS

There are 8 colored belt and 10 black belt levels in the American Eagle Cane Style.

They are as follows:

White Belt – 8th Gyup

Yellow Belt – 7th Gyup

Green Belt —6th Gyup

Blue Belt – 5th Gyup

Purple Belt – 4th Gyup

Brown Belt – 3rd Gyup (3rd Rank Brown Belt)

Brown Belt (1 black tip) – 2nd Gyup (2nd Rank Brown Belt)

Brown Belt (2 black tips) – 1st Gyup (1st Rank Brown Belt)

1st Degree Black Belt – 1st Dan

Tips are worn on the right side of the belt.

There are 10 Degrees of Black Belt. Only the founders or a single individual designated as the style's Headmaster's successor may hold the rank of 9th Degree Black Belt. There may only be one 10th Degree Black Belt and they are the Headmaster.

First Degree Black Belt: Solid, double wrap black belt

2nd – 8th Degree Black Belt: red tips approximately ¼ inch wide and equally spaced, beginning 1-2 inches from the end of the belt. ie) 2nd Dan = 2 tips, 3rd Dan = 3 tips, etc…Tips are worn on the right side of the belt.

9th – 10th Degree Black Belt: Name and "American Eagle Cane Style" embroidered on the belt. No tips to indicate rank. A student should know who these individuals are and what their position and rank are. 9th Dan is either an original style founder or designated successor. The 10th Dan is the Headmaster and belt indicates their ranks and title in blue.

KNOTS

Half-Kata knot: White through Purple Belt

Full Kata knot: brown, and all black belt levels

Procedure for Tying a Uniform Belt

Student ranks white through purple use this type of belt knot. Brown belts and black belts use what is referred to as a full kata knot in the American Eagle Cane Style.

1. Center the belt in front at your waist.

2. Carry ends around back behind you.

3. Continue bringing the belt ends around to your front.

4. Cross right end over the left end and tuck up under both layers in front of you. This now becomes your left end.

5. Cross ends as shown in diagram.

6. Cross left over right and tuck up through the hole created.

7. Pull ends to complete knot.

A square knot is formed. When extended out in front of you, the two ends of the belt should be the same length.

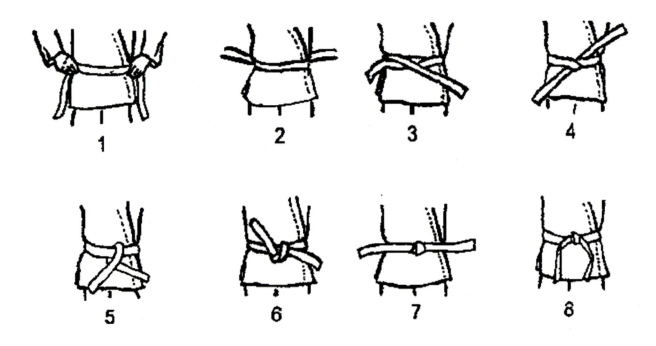

Uniform and Belt Etiquette

Keep your uniform clean and presentable. However, do not wash your belt. This has historic and practical signficance. Do not let your belt lay on the floor; instead, wrap or fold it, and carry it or put it in a bag for safe keeping. When promoted, keep your previous belts. You may wish to display them in your home on a special rack or store them. You may also wish to have a designated bag to carry your uniform to keep it clean. Only wear your uniform for official class training and desinated school events. Your uniform should be a source of pride.

Footwear

Whenever possible, students are expected to train in bare feet. This helps to strengthen the muscles of the feet, ankles, and legs for better balance and joint stability. It also provides a tactile sensation with the ground, allows for smoother movement in stance transitions, and offers other benefits. However, there are situations where it may be appropriate for a student to wear footwear. Check with your instructor regarding your personal situation. In these instances, the footwear should be white or black, only. It should also be designed for martial arts use, lacking tread on the ball of foot region to allow pivoting without injury to yourself or damage to the training floor. This footwear becomes part of your uniform, only to be worn in the training hall. If you need to train outdoors, separate footwear should be acquired and dedicated to this purpose.

Personal Items in Regards to Safety

Items such as jewelry and watches should not be worn with your uniform. While training they become a safety risk to your partner and yourself. For example, bracelets and necklaces can allow a partner's finger to be caught during self-defense. In addition, these personal items could be damaged during training.

These items may be permitted if they are of religious, marital, or medical importance. You need to inform your instructor of the reasons. And, in these instances, you will be required to keep necklaces within your t-shirt and other jewelry covered by cloth wrist bands or other protective means. Discuss this with your instructor if you have questions.

Frequently Asked Questions

What is the American Eagle Cane Style's logo?

The logo is the American Bald Eagle in flight grasping a cane in its talons.

What are the style's colors?

Red, white, and blue

Who are the style's founders?

The founders are Grandmaster Clifford Crandall, Jr., Headmaster Eric Stalloch, and Master Lynn Jessee. Learn more in the founders sections.

Who is the American Eagle Cane Style's first Headmaster?

Headmaster Eric Stalloch, 10th Dan.

What is the style's national and international heritage (roots)?

American Eagle Cane Style's historical roots are based on years of training and the certified and researchable lineage of its founders Grandmaster Crandall, Headmaster Stalloch, and Master Jessee. See the section of this textbook on the founders and cane history for more information. Based on their combined backgrounds, the American Eagle Cane System has the four primary national and international influences: American, Korean, Japanese, and Chinese.

Does this school and style have a website?
Yes. AmericanEagleCaneSystem.Com. In addition, the school is shared with the world through social media such as Facebook @AmericanEagleCaneSystem.

Cane Types Used in Classes

There are a wide variety of canes, and these are covered in more detail in chapter three. There are four types of canes that are commonly used by students. These canes are used for both their safety to the student and their partners. Parts of canes are also discussed more in chapter three.

Student Cane: a wooden cane approximately 36 inches in length with a shorter crook, rounded horn, and rubber tip. The diameter of the shaft is approximately 1 inch, which may include hand grips.

Instructor's Cane: this cane differs from the student cane in that its crook is longer and will encircle the neck of a partner to a greater degree. It often includes three sets of grips: near the crook, mid-shaft, and near the tip, or along the entire shaft. While referred to as an "instructor's cane," all levels of students may use this variety of cane.

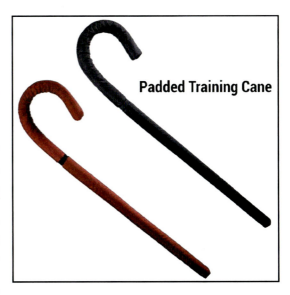

Padded Training Cane

Walking Staff: Black belt students may be seen using a cane with an elongated shaft with a total height between 5 and 6 feet. This is used for advanced techniques and the kata Briar Patch.

Padded Canes: these safety training canes contain a plastic core with a padded sheath. These are often used for 3-point sparring, advanced CTs, and other exercises.

Rules and Regulations

All students are responsible to know and follow the school's training rules:

1) Bowing is a sign of respect and is done before and after speaking with a Black Belt Instructor, upon entering or leaving the training hall, and to the highest ranked instructor on the floor upon entering the training hall.

2) Always show respect for all persons during training.

3) The use of profanity is not allowed.

4) No smoking, eating, chewing gum, or drinking in the training hall.

5) No talking during class.

6) Advise instructor before class starts if you must leave early.

7) Keep martial arts uniform clean and presentable. Only a white shirt without writing may be worn underneath white uniform jackets.

8) Do not strike or kick walls of training hall.

9) Street fighting is strictly forbidden unless it is in self-defense.

10) Coming to class late is perfectly acceptable if there is a schedule conflict. The students must fall in at the rear of the class until the class breaks for stretching or another class segment, and then when the class forms again they fall in at the normal place in formation.

11) Any member who tests for, or receives rank, in another martial arts school, other than this school must obtain written permission from the Headmaster.

12) Safety for one's partner, one's-self, and people surrounding the training space is the responsibility of the student; therefore, participants must use good control and be aware of their surroundings. Never use uncontrolled techniques while practicing self-defense or drills.

13) The student must keep their training cane in good repair, including a secured rubber tip.

14) Groin cups are suggested for males, and chest protectors are suggested for female participants in self-defense.

15) Only currently certified instructors may teach the style, certification must be renewed annually, and the current list of instructors may be found at AmericanEagleCaneSystem. Com

16) The American Martial Arts Institute and American Eagle Cane Style have the right to suspend any member whose conduct is not in keeping with the principles, policies, and rules of the school or whose actions would bring shame or adverse publicity to the school.

In addition, as a traditional school students are expected to learn the etiquette, much of which is subtle, for the style. Regarding watching classes and testings, note that no video or photography is permitted at any time during class or testing including the use of mobile devices, cameras, and personal computers / tablets. Guests are expected to use their cellular phones outside and to not talk while classes are in session. If you have any questions, speak with an instructor.

INSTRUCTOR STATUS

Great styles of martial arts can be lost or changed so much that they are no longer recognized as what they once were. Teaching is just as fulfilling, rewarding, and fun, as it is demanding, hard work and challenging. The act of teaching can become a hobby, a pastime or business. But in teaching a martial arts style, there is a responsibility to maintain that style's strengths and uniqueness. It is also important for the teachers to make sure that their students receive the same rewards from their training as the teachers did when they were students themselves. With this in mind, American Eagle Cane Style Instructors go through an educational program to help make this happen.

Teachers actively teach and they can explain one-on-one. For you to learn this style ultimately you need another, better skilled individual who has learned from a person whose knowledge has descended from the core of instructors who learned from the founders.

This individual now needs to:

1) Take your body structure into account regarding how you will execute certain moves.

2) Be aware of your mental and emotional state, such as your level of self-confidence, your personal concern as to how others see you and your ability to take correction.

3) Care about you as a person, especially your well-being and health. Therefore, to push you to new heights of success without risking your safety.

4) Be able to change terminology to meet your verbal understanding without changing the intent of the move or technique. Also to use terms and demonstration as the primary teaching tool rather than having to resort to physical contact with you.

With this understood, black belt instructors in this style are separately certified. Therefore, although all black belts are students, some have chosen the road to teach the style to others, which is truly different than doing it yourself.

As you study American Eagle Cane Style, look to your teachers to make the style come alive with the knowledge of its past and purpose for each of its actions. If you are studying American Eagle Cane Style from this textbook in an area far from where it is taught and wish to know more, seek out a certified instructor in this style. Instructors are certified yearly, which serves to maintain their accuracy in the areas of the style that are still growing. A small percentage of growth takes place in a style for each year it lives and matures, and as human beings change and evolve as well.

To become certified to teach in American Eagle Cane Style:

You must earn your black belt before you can enter the instructors' program. You must be a successful student of this style before you can walk the road to understand how to teach it. A black belt has to take the time to consider and understand what it means to actually be a black belt and to set the kind of example that helps others to learn and grow. Then they can, in writing, request admittance into the instructors' program. If accepted, they become an Instructor's Assistant. During this internship the apprentice instructor is taught the application of the moves and flow of the style as it pertains to people of different ages, sizes, and sex. Time is taken on the vocabulary of teaching this style for a word can have more than one meaning to more than one person. The apprenticeship time varies, but can be as short as three to six months, depending upon the student. One of the main aims is to pass on the American Eagle Cane Style with as much accuracy as possible. Each style of worth has a history and tradition, and its future worth depends on the consistency of carrying that information from one generation to another.

Instructors' may have students assigned under their direct supervision, and they will serve as their teacher and mentor; however, all are students of the Headmaster. In addition, an instructors' assistant may find that they wish to assist the instructors in the teaching of the style but do not wish to accept the responsibility of having students for whom they are directly accountable. Therefore, they may remain as assistants. Guidelines for the instructors' assistants program and instructors' program are available to black belts by speaking with their instructor.

CLASS STRUCTURE

Documentation such as this textbook is a powerful tool for helping instructors to maintatin consistency in the teaching of a traditional martial art style. Books, videos, and other forms of media are great resources but they are no substition for a qualified instructor. Books and videos do not teach; people teach. The American Eagle Cane Style is presented in an organized class structure, taught by a certified adult black belt instructor. For more information about classes and instructors contact the main office through AMAI-EagleStyle.Com. The following outline is of a typical American Eagle Cane Style class:

Bow In

> The class "falls in" belt rank order in rows

Meditation

> On insteps unless there is a physical limitation.

> See your instructor for alternative postures.

Stretching

Punches

> From a horse stance.

Kicks

Basic Forms

Forms (kata)

CTs

Additional Class Topic

> This segment may include additional practice in the segments list above, guard hand techniques, moving techniques, advanced techniques, three point sparring, and other areas.

Meditation

Bow Out

CHAPTER 3
CANE & GUARD HAND

STRETCHING
PROPER FIST
PROPER GUARD HAND
CANE TYPES

Warm-Up and Stretching

A thorough warm-up is essential before any exercise because it helps you prepare the cardiovascular and central nervous systems for a general increase in activity. It also helps prepare individual tissues such as muscles, tendons, and joints for the increased loading demands of movements that are specific to your activity. A good warm-up, therefore, should not only improve your performance but also reduce the risk of injury. The following exercises are performed at the beginning of each American Eagle Cane Style class.

1. Half Squats:

Hold your cane in a double shaft grip with both palms down, approximately shoulder width apart. With your feet about shoulder width apart stand as tall as you can and raise the cane up in front of you to about head height. Folding only at the hip joint, sit your hips back a short distance. Your torso will incline forward slightly in order to maintain balance as your hips move back, but do not allow your spine to round; the curve of your low back should stay the same for the whole movement. Do not allow the knees to come forward over your toes or inward toward each other. Bring your hips forward to stand erect again. Repeat 10 to 15 times.

2. Standing Twist:

Stand erect with your feet hip width apart. Hold your cane in a double shaft grip with both palms down, approximately shoulder width apart. Extend your arms straight in front of your body. Swing your arms (and the cane) from side to side, twisting at the waist. Keep your head and eyes facing front. Complete 10 repetitions.

3. Bend and Hold:

Stand erect with your feet hip width apart. Hold your cane in a double shaft grip with both palms down, approximately shoulder width apart. Extend your arms straight overhead. Bend at the waist to the left, stretching the muscles of the right side and the latissimus dorsi, then return to the starting position. Bend at the waist to the right, then return to the starting position. Bend slightly backwards, using extra caution so that you do not lose your balance, then return to the starting position. Bend forward, reaching the cane and both arms toward the floor, keeping the legs straight. Stand back up slowly, with caution, so that you don't lose your balance. With all four movements of this exercise, it is important to breathe. Exhaling slightly allows you to settle further into the stretch.

4. Cane Rotations:

Stand erect with your feet hip width apart. Grasping your cane in the center of the shaft, extend your right arm straight out in front of your body at shoulder height. Rotate the cane back and forth, palm up to palm down, or further if you can, through a comfortable range of motion. Do not perform this motion with power and "bounce off" the end range. The key is controlled movement. During the warm-up you are preparing the body's tissues by lightly loading them through the range. Complete 10 repetitions. Repeat with the left arm.

5. Wrist Stretches (2 Directions):

Place the cane on the floor next to you or hook it over the arm not being stretched. Stand erect with your feet hip width apart.

Wrist Stretch #1: Extend your right arm, palm toward the floor and bend your wrist so that the fingers point toward the floor. Wrap the palm of the left hand around the back of the knuckles of the extended right hand. Carefully draw the palm of the right hand back toward you, keeping the right arm straight. Hold the stretch for approximately 30 seconds. This stretches the wrist extensors, which are located on the top (knuckle side) of your forearm.

Wrist Stretch #2: Extend your right arm, palm toward the floor and bend your wrist so the fingers point to the ceiling. Wrap the palm of the left hand around the right palm, fingers, and thumb of the right hand. Carefully draw the right hand back toward you, keeping the right arm straight. Hold the stretch for approximately 30 seconds. This stretches the wrist flexors, which are located underneath your forearm (palm side).

Repeat these 2 stretches for the left arm.

6. Center Kick Stretch:

Pair with a partner approximately your height if possible, and stand with your back to the wall for support. Place your cane on the ground next to you, or if necessary, hold it with the tip on the floor (on the side opposite your partner) for added support. Bring your right knee up and extend your leg directly out in front of your body with the ball of the foot pressed forward and the toes pulled back. Your partner stands on the outside of the leg being stretched and assists by supporting the stretching leg under the heel with one hand. They place their other hand over your knee to keep the knee locked and to feel for any strain or vibration in the knee during the stretch. Raise the leg until you feel a slight stretch and hold for approximately 30 seconds, or until the instructor tells you to set it down. Throughout the stretch, the student who is assisting must be alert for any loss of balance in their partner and be prepared to lower their leg immediately. Repeat this stretch with the opposite leg. Switch partners to stretch both the right and left sides of the second partner.

THE GUARD POSITION

In the American Eagle Cane Style, when you are holding your cane in one hand, the opposite (empty) hand is often referred to as the *guard hand*. When it is not occupied with blocking, striking, or reinforcing the shaft of the cane, it should be held in the guard position. The guard position is formed by placing your open hand in a position floating a few inches in front of your chest, palm facing in. The hand is rigid with the extended fingers held tightly together. The thumb is also held tight to the side of the hand, not open or folded under the palm. The wrist should be straight.

The palm-in position protects the sensitive structures of the palm side of the wrist such as arteries and flexor tendons which allow you to close your hand to grip. This can be important when defending against an attack with a bladed weapon.

In the guard position, the hand should never be relaxed or resting on your chest. This is an active posture where the hand is available and ready to block, strike, or assume a reinforced or double shaft grip at any moment in time.

Making a Proper Fist

How to make a proper fist may seem obvious to some, but it is a question often asked by many new martial arts students. When talking to a trained martial artist or boxer, you might find two or perhaps three acceptable ways. However, there is one that is recommended most because of its safety for the thumb and the effective use of the hand as a striking tool. The following is that method and it is the process used by students of the American Eagle style.

FIRST: Put your hand palm up with your fingers flat out and thumb out to the side. Now fold your fingers (or curl) them back onto themselves and into the palm of your hand.

Note: Never put your thumb in the center of your hand and fold your fingers over it. To strike with your hand in this structure is to risk breaking or dislocating your thumb upon hand impact.

SECOND: Now that the fingers are closed and tight, place your thumb over the first two fingers.

THIRD: The hand is now closed and the fingers that make up the knuckles that you will strike with are reinforced by the thumb. When you punch, you should intend on striking with the first two knuckles of your hand.

  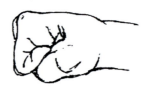 

CANE TYPES

Canes are available in diverse styles, materials, and lengths, which may serve many purposes. These canes can range from the collapsible aluminum variety intended for medical support to ornate carved hardwoods trimmed with gold and expensive jewels as a fashion accessory. The vast multitude of canes historically, artistically, and functionally is so great that entire books have been written, private and public collections have been organized, and a complete discussion is not possible here. What the American Eagle Cane Stylist should recognize is the enormity of the topic.

Parts of the Cane

There are four primary cane parts in the American Eagle Cane Style. These include the tip, shaft, crook, and horn. Each of these areas is available in a variety of styles, which are discussed in more detail below. As these areas change, they can alter the effectiveness of particular techniques, pose additional considerations regarding safety for your partner and yourself, change how the cane is properly cared for, and apply different stresses to your body (especially joints) based on weights and grips. For instance, a low density wood with a small diameter shaft may not be suitable for bagwork as it could break, damaging the cane and putting others at risk in a number of ways, including projectile fragments. While a cane with a highly curved crook and pointed horn may not be the appropriate to use with a partner. Below you will find some of the cane features available, types of canes, and cane accessories. There are dozens of books hundreds of pages long dedicated to different types of canes. This is only intended to give you an overview of the most common types you might encounter in your training. In addition, you should seek out your instructor and ask questions regarding the cane types and their appropriate use.

Tips

The tip is the part of the cane in contact with the floor. This is typically composed of rubber or similar polymer and is intended to generate friction with the ground and provide stability through the shaft. A decorative ring of brass or copper is often found above the tip as decorative ornamentation and as a collar which adds strength at this point of stress. The tip also serves other functions. It protects the exposed end of the cane's wood from chipping and splitting. It protects your partner from this free edge which can often be sharp from where it was cut to length. In addition, for tip-end impacts the friction of the tip will hold firm to the point of contact with the target, transferring the energy of the block or strike.

There are additional tips available. These include tri- and quad-cane designs which feature multiple tips branching from the end of the shaft for an increased base of support. White canes used by individuals who are blind or visually impaired may feature specialized tips used for sweeping their surroundings. These can include mushroom tips, standard tips, roller tips, teardrop tips, and others. There are also flat metal tips with a pivoting joint similar to what you would find on the legs of a school chair or desk. There are even wheels that attach to the end of a cane.

The tip may also feature accessory devices such as an ice gripper for inclement weather. The three most common varieties are: 1) a metal brace secured around the end of the shaft that contains a hinge and end with serrations which pivots beneath the tip, 2) a rubber tip with a spike that can swivel down to penetrate the icy surface, and 3) an spike that is integral to the shaft which is deployed by means of a lever and which emerges from the tip.

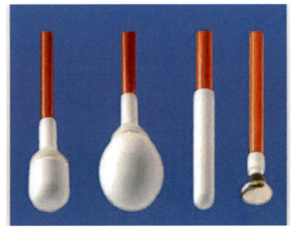

Shaft

The shaft is the length of the cane which extends from the tip to the crook or grip. The shaft may be metal, polymer, carbon fiber, or a variety of wood species. It may be rigid, collapsible, foldable, or retractable. Generally, the shaft of the cane is straight; however, there are some ergonomic designs which feature curvature. The length of the shaft averages between 29 and 40 inches depending on the user's height and needs. There is a difference between sizing a cane for daily use as a medical device and for purely training purposes. For daily use, you should consult a physician who is familiar with your needs and who is qualified to give this advice. For training purposes, you must first answer the question, will the cane be primarily used with or without footwear. When

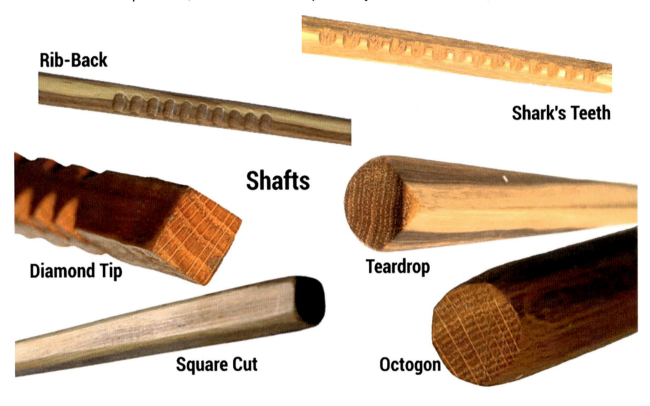

Rib-Back

Shark's Teeth

Shafts

Diamond Tip

Teardrop

Square Cut

Octogon

sizing your cane for this purpose, you should measure the cane accordingly because the extra height imparted by your footwear will differ from barefoot. See your instructor to learn more about sizing the cane.

American Eagle Cane Stylists most commonly use a wooden cane made from oak or hickory. Many other wood types are available including hickory heart wood, maple, walnut, and cherry to name a few. No two wood canes are identical. The conditions under which the wood grew, the time of year it was harvested, and how it was treated during crafting can all lead to vary different densities and weights. There are also canes constructed from rattan or hollow bamboo.

The diameter of the shaft can also vary. Typically, an American Eagle Cane Stylist utilizes a one-inch diameter shaft; however, 3/4 and 7/8 inch diameters are also common in circumstances where the instructor desires the student to use a cane with less weight or load.

Occasionally, different regions of the shaft will be referred to. This can include the face, sides, striking surface, grip, mid-shaft, and end-grip. There are many acceptable ways to grasp a cane. In the American Eagle Cane Style, we identify the grips and parts of the cane from a standard position. This is with the hand resting on top of the crook with the horn posterior and the tip on the ground. In this position, we imagine the shaft as a rectangular block, instead of round. The front of the shaft is referred to as the face, the posterior shaft is the striking surface, and the right and left surfaces are the sides. Sliding the hand forward and down the shaft, the hand is now in a natural grip. This area of the shaft is the grip, the middle of the cane is the mid-shaft, and the far end approximately two to three fist distances from the tip is the end-grip. These regions of the shaft can have various diameters, grips, and shapes.

The shaft of the cane can also have a variety of shapes and features. Shapes include round, oval, teardrop, octagonal, square-cut, diamond tip, and others. Features include grips, band-holders, notches, and others. The typical cane is round with a consistent diameter the length of the shaft and continuing through the crook. Oval refers to a

High Gloss Tung Oil

Organic Tung Oil

Black Dye with Tung Oil

shaft with an elliptical cross-section. A tear drop shaft is round on the face but has flat tapered sides which come to a ridge along the striking surface; the teardrop can span the entire length of the shaft or only along a segment. Square-cut and diamond-tip are similar in that they both have four flat sides with some beveling at their edges. However, in cross section, the square-tip has a flat face, sides, and striking surface; whereas, the diamond-tip has its flat surfaces at a forty-five degree angle from the square-cut variety with its edges facing to the front, sides, and back. As the names suggest, one appears as a square and the other a diamond in cross section. Octagonal appears as an octagon in cross section. There are many other shaft shapes, but these above are most common.

Grips on Shaft

Grips on Crook

Grips are small oval shaped indentations carved into the shaft that increase surface area and allow the hands to grasp the cane more securely. They can vary in depth, spacing, angle, and location. They may appear at the grip, mid-shaft, end-grip, along the entire shaft, or in varying combinations. Band holders are smooth deeper indentations intended to be used with an elastic physical therapy tubing. Notches similar in design to grips but are deeper and create raised ridges can be used in certain techniques in conjunction with pressure points. Other features of canes can be decorative including spiral patterns, carved patterns or images, laser engraving and more.

It is also important to note that shafts can be highly variable when they are hand crafted from branches, found wood, composite woods, and by other means.

Open Crook

Closed Crook

Crook

The crook is the curved portion of the cane at the end of the shaft opposite from the tip. When a cane possesses a crook it may be commonly referred to as a c-cane or crook cane. The crook is one type of cane grip or handle. The crook can have a variety of lengths and curvatures. In the American Eagle Cane Style, the student cane has a shorter crook with a more broadly curved crook to minimize how it hooks parts of the body, especially the neck. An instructor's cane has a longer crook that bends inward more as it approaches the horn. Other crooks may be narrower or more tightly curved.

The crook may also feature a beveled edge along the crook where it is continuous with the face of the shaft, and this is sometimes also referred to as a striking edge. Crooks can also have other decorative features.

Other grip or handle styles include the orthopedic grip, pistol grip, knob handle, derby, fritz, off-set, ergonomic, t-top, custom carved, and more. These handles serve a variety of purposes. The majority of American Eagle Cane Style techniques can be executed with these grips; however, there are some techniques that require a crook.

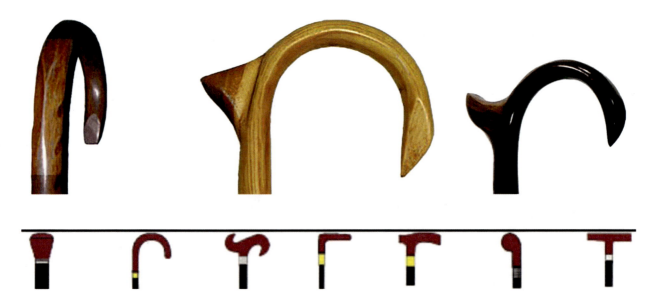

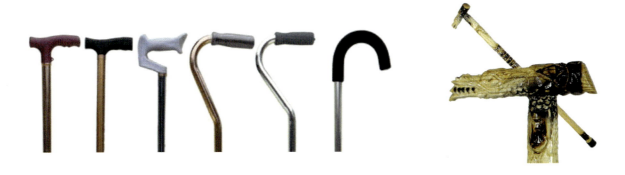

Horns

Horns are sometimes referred to as the beak. A horn is where the crook terminates and can be round, chisel tipped, pointed, and other shapes. A chisel tip is an oblique angle cut at the end of the crook and it can be angled inward or outward. A pointed horn can vary from needle-sharp to gently round. Even the horn can feature decorative features.

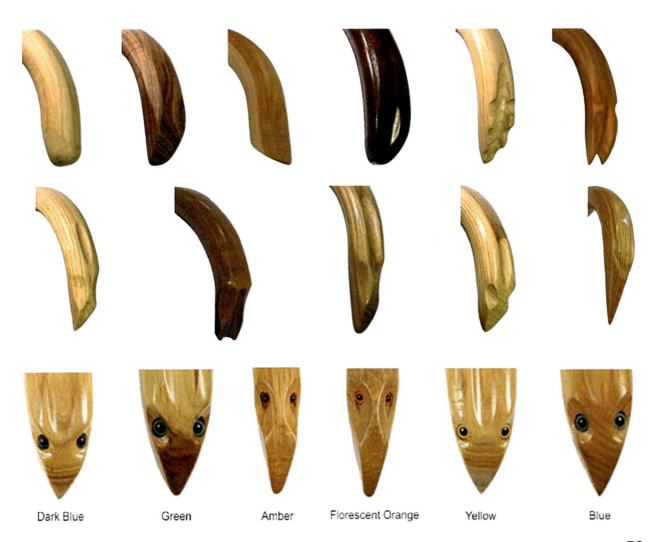

| Dark Blue | Green | Amber | Florescent Orange | Yellow | Blue |

Finishes

Wooden canes can have a variety of finishes. For the protection of the wood and to maintain the curvature of the crook, mineral oil is an essential treatment. Proper cane care involves periodic application of mineral oils. In addition, canes can be stained, painted, or glossed with furniture polish.

Walking Staffs

A walking staff can feature all of the same features as a cane, but it's total shaft length is longer, typically between four and six feet. If it possesses a crook it may commonly be referred to as a Bo-Cane, BoKane, or Sheppard's Crook. Walking staffs may include the addition of other features including a metal, chisel-shaped tip, a compass, paracord grips, and more.

Master Bokane

Mini Canes

A walking cane with significantly shorter staff is often referred to as a mini-cane and can be useful for both self-defense techniques and practice of full-length cane techniques. Often training with a cane requires a degree of open space. Whether it is to the size of a room or the number of students training on the floor, a mini-cane allows for the majority of full-length cane techniques to be practiced with less space.

White Canes

The white cane is most often identified as adaptive equipment for individuals who are blind or visually impaired, and it was introduced after World War I. The white cane is also called the Hoover cane, long cane, white stick, and typhlo-cane. They may be straight or collapsible and are typically composed of lightweight materials such as aluminum, carbon-fibers, or

graphite reinforced polymers. The length can vary but typically spans from the floor to the user's sternum when held vertically. What constitutes a white cane is actually its coloration, being white for the length with one or more red bands, and it is typically reflective so that drivers see the pedestrian who is utilizing it. The collapsible variety typically has four interlocking segments with an elastic cord running through the hollow center to keep the segments together in order when folded, and to provide tension through the length when assembled. Shorter versions of the white cane are often referred to as guide canes, where a heavier, more robust cane may be called a support cane. In some countries a green cane indicates low-vision, whereas the white can indicates lack of sight.

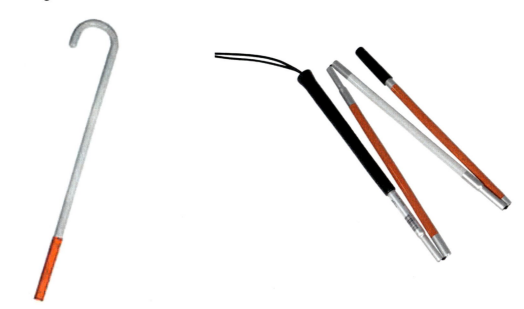

Padded Canes

Padded Training Cane

Padded training canes are typically composed of a plastic or polymer core surrounded by padding and an outer material that is non-abrasive. They are used in practice when a lighter cane may reduce the stress on the joints, for bagwork, 3-point sparring, self-defense, and other training activities.

Umbrellas and Tools at Hand

In addition to the vast diversity of canes, umbrellas and other tools can be effective tools for personal protection, utilizing many of the same techniques and concepts of the cane. Full length and short collapsible umbrellas are the most analogous to cane techniques and can be carried while you are traveling. Short dowels, broom handles, dowels, ice-scrapers, golf clubs, field hockey sticks, tennis rackets, and nearly any rigid item of similar length, weight, and diameter as a cane can be used. Techniques will need to be altered to fit the tool and situation. Even a rolled up magazine or pencil provides enough rigidity for a large number of techniques to adapt from the cane.

Accessories

The use of canes can be further enhanced through various accessories. These can include cane clips to secure them to a wheel-chair, walker, wall, or table where you commonly sit. These clips come in many styles but hold the cane so that it can be easily released and used. Ice grippers allow the cane better support in slippery environmental conditions and were discussed above in the section on tips. Cane racks, stands, and storage cases protect the cane from damage and warping. Wrist straps can be added and are typically secured near the crook end.

Gadget Canes

It is important to note that canes exist with variety of other features that one might not commonly associate with a cane. Many of these devices are illegal based on national, state, and local laws, and you should consult these statutes before obtaining or using one. These are often referred to as gadget canes. They can include hidden swords, components which classify them as a firearm, concealed compartments, levers and attachments which extend to create make-shift chairs, and many more.

CARING FOR YOUR CANE

Just like any other quality tool, your cane needs maintenance and care. With use the surface of your cane will get dirty simply from the oils on your hand. Occasionally, you will need to "clean" your cane to keep it looking good. The following information is provided by Cane Masters, our preferred provider of quality training canes.

Procedure for canes that do NOT have a tung oil finish:

- Wipe your cane down with a soft cloth (good terry-cloth) and mineral oil.
- Sand the cane with 400 grit wet/dry sandpaper. Be sure to pay attention to the grips on the shaft.
- Wipe the cane again with your cloth and mineral oil.
- Sand the cane with 600 grit wet/dry sandpaper.
- Wipe the cane once more with your cloth and mineral oil.
- At this point, your cane will be clean and well "fed" with mineral oil. Finish the job by wiping off the excess mineral oil, or you can go one step further by "polishing" the cane with 1000-1500 grit wet/dry sandpaper and mineral oil. Just remember to complete the procedure by wiping off any excess mineral oil.
- The process to clean the surface of a tung oiled cane is somewhat similar:
- Wipe the cane down with a soft cloth and mineral oil
- Lightly sand with 1000-1500 grit wet/dry sandpaper.
- Wipe off the excess mineral oil and give it a hardy rubdown with your cloth.
- Do not dry sand your cane unless you want to refinish it; always use mineral oil!

Applying a High Gloss Tung Oil Finish

Tung Oil Treatment is different in application than other methods you might be familiar with. The following is a description, recommended by Cane Masters, for finishing or re-finishing* your cane:

1. Wipe down your cane with mineral oil (be sure to ALWAYS apply mineral to your cane first before sanding it!)

2. Sand with 600 grit wet/dry sand paper.

3. Wipe off any residue.

4. Apply a coat of tung oil with a rag and let dry overnight

5. Apply another coat of tung oil and let dry overnight.

6. Wipe down cane with mineral oil.

7. Sand lightly with 600 grit wet/dry sand paper.

8. Wipe off any residue

9. Apply a coat of tung oil and let dry overnight.

10. Repeat steps 6-9 three more times

11. Wipe down cane with mineral oil

12. Sand with 1200 or 1500 grit wet/dry sand paper

13. Wipe off any residue

14. Apply tung oil and let dry overnight.

15. Repeat steps 11-14 once more.

16. Repeat steps 11-13 and enjoy your beautifully finished cane!

*Note: If you are refinishing your existing tung oil treatment, you will first need to strip off the existing finish with a rougher grit sand paper (320).

To keep your finished cane looking great, simply wipe down with mineral oil and give it an occasional sanding with 1200 or 1500 grit wet/dry sand paper (with mineral oil) to remove any dirt.

Storing your Cane

The cane's shaft can warp and the crook can open wider over time if not properly cared for and stored. One of the best ways to store a cane is to lay it flat on the floor or on a shelf if possible, where the entire length is supported with a firm surface. They can also be stored vertically, secured to a wall with clips or upright in a stand which keeps it in a vertical alignment. Leaning a cane up against a wall creates an angle that over time will lead to warping. There are also storage cases available to secure the cane. Proper maintenance with mineral oil should prevent the crook from straightening.

Sizing Your Cane

It is easiest to get an accurate length for your cane if you have somebody else to help you take the measurement.

To measure yourself for a cane, stand on a flat surface with your shoes on and stand up straight. Let your arms hang free and have somebody measure you from the ground up to where your wrist bends.

Add one inch to that measurement for an accurate cane length. Remember, if in doubt, cut your cane an extra inch or two longer from your measurement.

CHAPTER 4
STANCES

STANCES

STANCES

Stances are the basic foundation for the performance of all of your techniques. Placing your feet in the proper position to handle the movement and forces upon your body as you execute blocks and strikes is essential to maintaining your balance and stability as well as allowing you to bring power to your cane techniques.

In the American Eagle Cane Style, the cane can act as part of your foundation by expanding your base of support and providing additional stability. This is especially useful when only one foot is in contact with the ground, such as during the crane stance or for kicks. The cane can act as an additional "leg" or point of support which changes or expands your center of gravity to be distributed between the cane and your supporting leg.

Similarly, if you are seated in a chair or wheelchair, your hips and pelvis must be positioned and braced accordingly to create the stable foundation needed for effective techniques during cane training. Keep in mind that many factors such as height, flexibility, and your individual physical structure may affect your stances, causing them to look slightly different than what is pictured here. Your American Eagle Cane Style instructor will work with you as an individual, including taking into consideration any physical limitations you may have, to determine what is correct for you.

CHUMBI (READY STANCE)

Starting with your cane in the holstered position under your right arm and upon the command "Chumbi," the left foot comes in to touch the right foot and your left (empty hand) fist is raised to chest level palm in. Your left foot then steps back out so that the feet are parallel, pointing forward, and about hip width apart. As the left foot sets down, both hands are thrust downward in front of you. Your right hand maintains its grip on the crook of the cane. In the finished position the palm side of your hands are facing toward your body, about a fist distance in front of you, and 2 to 3 inches apart from each other. Chumbi is a very formal preparatory stance. Do not move in Chumbi, be focused and ready for the next command.

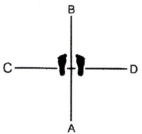

NATURAL STANCE

In the natural stance one foot is slightly ahead of the other. Both feet are pointed straight ahead and your weight is distributed equally between them. The natural stance is sometimes called a "standing stance" and it allows you to use your hips during cane techniques such as striking by shifting them slightly.

FRONT STANCE

In a front stance the feet are about shoulder width apart and the front foot is about two shoulder widths in front of the back foot. Both feet are pointing straight ahead and the weight distribution is approximately 60% of your weight on the front leg and 40% of your weight on the back leg. This weight distribution is the same whether the cane is in your right or left hand. Your front knee is bent so that your lower leg is perpendicular to the ground. Your back leg should be locked with no bend in the knee.

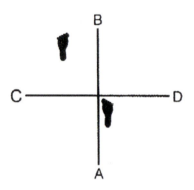

BACK STANCE

In a back stance the feet will be at right angles to each other with the front foot pointed toward the front and the back foot pointed toward the side. The heels should be

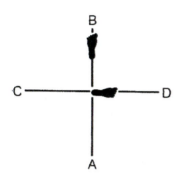

lined up with each other and about two shoulder widths apart. The weight distribution is approximately 70% of your weight on the back leg and 30% of your weight on the front leg. The back leg is bent so that the hip, knee, and ankle are aligned. The front knee is slightly bent. In this stance your hips and upper body will face to one side. This can influence which hand holds the cane for certain techniques, or the directionality of your grip for techniques such as the lunge strike.

HORSE STANCE

In a horse stance your feet are pointed straight ahead and approximately two shoulder widths apart. The knees are bent and pushed out, and the hips are pushed back in line with the heels. Your weight is distributed equally on both legs. Because of the wide base of support, this is a very stable stance ideal for practicing cane techniques.

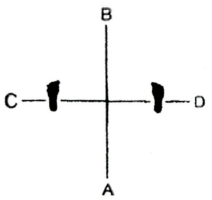

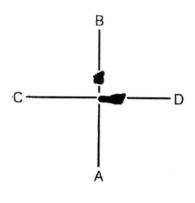

CAT STANCE

In a cat stance your feet will be at right angles to each other with the front foot pointed straight ahead and the back foot pointed toward the side. Raise the front heel so that only the ball of your foot and toes are touching the ground. Traditionally, the distance between your feet is such that if you set the front heel down from its cocked position your heels will touch each other. If they are at a greater distance away from each other, it is sometimes called a "tiger stance." Both knees are slightly bent and most of your weight is on your back leg. Because the base of support for this stance is small, the cat stance may challenge your balance. Your cane may be used as a "third leg" to assist you by setting the tip on the floor for support.

CRANE STANCE

A crane stance is a one legged posture with the other leg raised so that the foot is near the knee of the supporting leg. There are a variety of ways to perform the crane stance.

Wrapped/Tucked Instep style- the instep of the raised foot is wrapped around the back of the supporting knee, resting on the top of the calf. Your supporting knee should be slightly bent.

Side Kick style- the raised foot assumes a side kick posture with the side of the foot (blade) extended and the toes pulled back. The foot may float next to the supporting knee or touch it. The raised knee is angled outward toward the target. Your supporting knee should be slightly bent.

Because of its single-leg support, the crane stance is among the most difficult foundational stances of the American Eagle Cane Style regarding balance. Use your cane to assist you if needed by placing the tip of the cane on the floor for an additional point of support.

X-STANCE

The X-stance tends to be a transitional stance used for moving from one technique to another. It may also be used when jumping or skipping forward to close distance quickly to strike or block with your cane. In the X-stance one foot will be crossed in front or behind the other with only the ball of the foot and toes of the advancing foot touching the ground. The flat foot will bear most of your weight.

KIHONDACHI

This traditional Japanese stance is done at the black belt levels; for example, it occurs in the kata Valley.

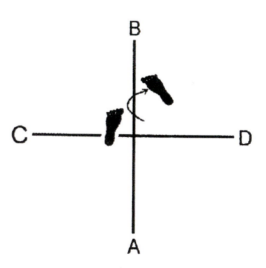

CHAPTER 5
GRIPS

GRIPS

GRIPS

The following are some of the most common grips used in the American Eagle Cane Style. How you hold your cane is important because it determines what techniques are available for you to use during training, or what techniques can be used for a counter or follow-up technique during self-defense practice. The American Eagle Cane Style teaches a multitude of effective techniques that can be performed from each grip.

CROOK GRIP

When the tip of the cane is resting on the floor and your hand is grasping the crook, if the horn is facing toward the back it is referred to as a crook grip. When the cane is held with a crook grip in the chamber position it will be <u>horn-down</u>. Also, if the shaft of the cane is laying across the back of the arm with the horn facing away, this is still a crook grip, because the cane hasn't left its position. This grip can be used for cane punches from the chambered position, or techniques that allow rotation of the crook within your grasp, such as swing strikes, figure-8's, side twirls, and clearing techniques.

REVERSE CROOK GRIP

When the tip of the cane is resting on the floor and your hand is grasping the crook, if the horn is facing forward it is referred to as a reverse crook grip. When the cane is held with a reverse crook grip in the chambered position it will be <u>horn-up</u>. Also, if the shaft of the cane is laying across the back of the arm with the horn facing toward you, this is still a reverse crook grip because the cane hasn't left its position. This grip can be used for cane punches from the chambered position, or techniques that allow rotation of the crook within your grasp, such as swing strikes, figure-8's, and clearing techniques.

NATURAL GRIP

The natural grip refers to grasping the cane shaft near the crook end, at the level approximately across from the end of the horn, depending on the type of cane you have and the length of the horn. Some canes are equipped with notches ("grips") in this area to help you hold your cane more securely. The hand should be down far enough so that it is only on the straight part of the shaft without the palm along the curvature of the crook. Also, when the fingers are not within the curvature of the horn, this allows for the weight of the crook to be a counter balance and give more space for hooking techniques. This is a common grip for many different blocks and strikes, and the most common grip used for the American Eagle Cane Style basic forms.

MIDSHAFT GRIP

The midshaft grip refers to holding the cane by the middle of the shaft with the horn facing away from you. The midshaft grip is used for blocking and striking with the crook end of the cane, which allows for follow-up techniques with the crook or horn: hooking with the crook around a limb or neck, or taking advantage of the penetrating potential of the horn during pulling motions.

REVERSE MIDSHAFT GRIP

The reverse midshaft grip refers to holding the cane by the middle of the shaft with the horn facing you. This is sometimes referred to as a "Punch Grip," because it can be used for Vertical, Horizontal, and Diagonal punches. It can also be used for striking with the back of the crook.

DOUBLE-SHAFT GRIP

A double-shaft grip refers to both hands closed on the shaft of the cane palm-down to execute a strike or a block. One benefit to the double-shaft shaft grip is that it allows maximum power to be generated from both arms.

END GRIP

Holding the cane near the tip end of the shaft is useful when striking with the crook end of the cane. Crook strikes make available many follow-up techniques that utilize the crook for hooking and controlling, or throwing an assailant. You may hold the tip end with one or two hands. Your grip should be 1-2 fist distances from the tip. When using two hands to execute a crook strike, the supporting hand grips below the main hand controlling the cane.

CHAPTER 6
GUARD HAND

PUNCHES
GUARD HAND TECHNIQUES

Guard Hand Techniques

The cane is a versatile tool which extends the mind and body of the American Eagle Cane Stylist. The guard hand and other empty –hand body parts are also important martial arts weapons. Below you will find more information about some of the empty-hand techniques that can be used in conjunction with the cane.

Center Punch

The center punch or lunge punch involves traditional punching with the added power of the cane in one hand. Punches may be done from a horse stance or while moving forward. From your defensive posture you will chamber the cane to your right side, horn down. Step forward with your right foot and throw the right hand which is holding the cane by the top of the crook with the crook horn up. Guide the cane straight out in front of you with the length of the cane parallel to the floor. With your next step (left foot forward) you will drive your left fist, which is palm up near the top of your hip, straight out while rotating the palm down as it moves and finishes its punch. Simultaneously the cane has flowed straight back to your right chamber, crook horn up. Upon your next right step the right hand holding the cane will execute the punch while the left hand will move back into the left chamber, rotating to stop palm up near the left upper hip. All of these punches with and without the cane are directed to an imaginary solar plexus target in front of you. Striking is done with the first two knuckles of the closed fist for the empty hand, and with all four knuckles as they are vertical holding the cane crook. When puches are executed from a horse stance without stepping as in single, double, and triple punches, the command "Prepare for Punches" is given. Step your left foot out into a horse stance and raise the left arm, extended. To switch hands, the command "Switch Hands" is given.

If you are not holding your cane and are practicing center punches the following would be done. The punch is released from the chamber on the first count or step. The punch comes from the same side as the leading leg, which in this case is the right side. As you step forward the right hand that was in the chamber is now released and sent straight out to the solar plexus area in front of you. Your right arm in this case should slide against your body so that you do not lead with your elbow. Striking is done with the first two knuckles, and the wrist should be flat.

Understanding the Fundamentals of
Guard Hand Techniques

You should learn the following six empty-hand basic form techniques without the use of your cane. Understanding them will assist you when you do use your cane and assist you in balancing your body and movements when the cane is in one hand. Let's go over the six fundament empty-hand moves that will play a foundation and fundamental role in your Cane Basic Forms and general self-defense.

Down Block - Front Stance: This empty hand basic form uses both arms when performed without the cane in one hand. From your chumbi position step forward into a left front stance. Your left arm should first go to your right shoulder and then slide down your right arm, which has been placed diagonally across the front of your body. As the left arm reaches the wrist of the right arm, pull the right hand back into the chamber just about belt level and finish pushing your left arm down and over your left thigh. (Note this basic form does not have to start with chumbi.)

Center Block – Front Stance: Again you will move into a front stance and this time the blocking arm will be placed down in front of you. The move of the block is a half circle up across the center of your body. You will be able to execute this motion by placing the blocking arm down just as you start to move.

High Block – Front Stance: Again you will be in a front stance with the weight distribution as 60/40, having your front leg bent at the knee and perpendicular to the floor. The blocking arm is again brought down to the lower part of your body and then, with the other arm acting as a cross-chest guard on the inside, you bring the blocking hand up on the outside (closed fist with palm facing your face), leading with the fist, then the wrist, and then the elbow. This straight upward motion changes as the fist passes your eyes, and the blocking hand now pivots outwardly which will rotate your elbow and create an angle to the competed block. This will not only protect your head but also safeguard your arm from the impact that you are blocking from. As your elbow passes the cross-chest guarding hand, it is snapped back into the chamber.

Outside Block – Horse Stance: Outside block can be done in a front stance or back stance, but it is very effective in the horse stance. Because of this you will see it as a basic empty-hand movement in a horse stance more often.

This is done in a horse stance which is a 50/50 weight distribution. The technique is a 45° angled arm with a closed fist. The first stage is a step into the horse stance with the blocking arm left behind you and cocked from the outside. Once you are stable into the horse stance, you swing the blocking arm forward into position with the knuckles of the blocking arm now facing the direction of the attacker. The arm should have approximately one fist distance from the elbow to your rib cage and the fist should be at shoulder level.

Knife Hand Block – Back Stance: Again this is done in a back stance but could be done in a front stance or horse stance. Although each technique has its own level of difficulty, the knife hand block combines different concerns at the same time which makes this one of the more challenging basic forms for beginners in any traditional martial arts style. Things to keep in mind: the knife hand should be straight at the wrist, making the elbow of the arm to the tips of the fingers one straight tool for blocking. If it is a right knife hand block, the right hand will start up by the left side of your face while the left hand will start extended from the arm at about mid-waist and straight back behind you. They move in unison and the left hand will circle up, out and then in to cover your solar plexus with the edge of the palm area. At the same time the right hand will pivot from the elbow, which you do not lift, and end up out in front of you at about a 45° angle with the blade angled toward the outside of your body.

When holding your cane you will have a guard hand floating across the center of your upper chest. This guard hand will move into a knife hand block from this position.

Side Punch – Horse Stance: Horse stance is the most common foot foundation for a side punch in the fundamentals of traditional martial arts. Moving in your horse stance this time you are punching in the direction that you are moving. To do this you first place your punching handd in the chamber, palm-up. As you step into a firm horse stance, you deliver the right punch, making sure that the elbow is behind the hand at all times. The other hand is quickly pulled back into the left chamber.

Guard Hand Drills

Guard hand techniques may be drilled through repetition in a variety of manners. Two of the most common methods involve movement forward and backward through the training space in a manner similar to basic forms.

The first method utilizes the cane in a chambered crook grip and is often referred to as A/B drills. The "A" portion of the drill is the execution of the guard hand technique. If the guard hand is the left hand, then this is performed in a left stance. If the guard hand is the right hand, then this is performed in a right stance. The "B" portion of the drill is a step forward into the same stance with both hands in the chambers. Movement forward may include any number of steps until the instructor gives the command to turn around. Turning around is the same as basic forms. Once turned around, the lead leg determines if you are in an "A" or "B" position. A second method to practice guard hand techniques is without the use of the cane, and they occur in the same manner as basic forms. Other methods for practicing drills are presented in class under the direction of an instructor.

Example 1.1

Example 1.2

Example 1.3

Example 1.4

Example 1.5

Example 1.6

Example 1.7

Example 1.8

Example 1.9

Example 1.10

Example 1: Guard Hand High Block Drill A/B Sets

1.1: Chumbi

1.2 : "A": Step forward and execute the guard hand technique. In this case, a high block.

1.3 : "B": Step forward and chamber the guard hand with a proper fist.

1.4-1.5: Another A and B set demonstrated.

1.6: Turn around. Because the lead leg is same side as the guard hand, execute the high blok again.

1.7-1.10: The high block performed again in A/B sets including turning around.

Example 2.1

Example 2.2

Example 2.3

Example 2.4

Example 2.5

Example 2.6

Example 2: Side Punch Guard Hand Technique A/B Sets

2.1: Chumbi

2.2 : "A": Step forward in a horse stance and execute a side punch.

2.3 : "B": Step forward in a horse stance and chamber the guard hand.

2.4 -2.6: Another A/B set, then looking to turn around in the horse stance.

2.7: Because the lead leg is the same side as the guard hand, a punch is executed in place.

2.8-2.10: Demonstration of another A/B set leading up to preparing to turn around.

Example 2.7

Example 2.8

Example 2.9

Example 2.10

Side Punch A/ B Sets Transitions

Pictures 3.1-3.6: An example of a side punch being demonstrated to show the proper alignment of the elbow behind the fist throughout the flow of the technique.

Example 3.1

Example 3.2

Example 3.3

Example 3.4

Example 3.5

Example 3.6

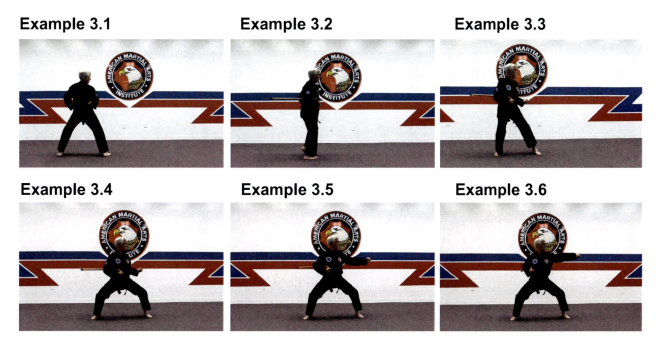

Basic Kicks

Keep in mind that each basic kick may be used in more than one way or in different stances. The following is a description of the basic kicks as they are normally done in a regular class structure. Also realize that for each kick the hands and arms should be kept in a proper guard position.

Preparing for Kicking

To prepare for kicking, first go into a ready stance with the cane chambered with a crook grip under your right arm. The command "Prepare for Kicks" will be given. From this position you step forward with your left leg into a front left stance. At the same time, raise your left hand into a guard hand position and allow the crook of the cane to rotate in the palm of your right hand so the tip rests on the floor to your right side. From this position most kicks can be executed; however, the grip can also be switched to guard position with both hands on the cane.

Center Kick

From a front stance, the back leg executes the kick by first raising the knee upwards as high as possible to the front. At this point, the foot should be directly under the knee with the toes pulled back and the ball of the foot extended downwards. The leg is then extended "penetrating" with the ball of the foot in a forward motion until the knee is locked. The leg is recocked in the reverse motion with the knee high and then replaced into its front stance. The photographs below depict the range of heights that you should be able to work within, but the knee is always cocked high, even for a low kick. When the cane is used for support, it may be used on either side of the body.

Side Kick to the Side

From a front stance raise the back leg bringing the knee up in front as high as possible. At this point, the foot will be pulled upward and the lower leg will slightly tilt inward so the knee is pointing towards the outside of the body (the target area). Extend the kicking leg to the outside so that the foot follows a straight line to its target. Before the knee locks completely, pivot on the ball of the supporting foot, directing the heel of that foot towards the target and rotate the hips into the kick, striking the target with the blade of the foot. Recock the kick in the reverse motion and place the foot back into its front stance. When the cane is used for support, it is most commonly on opposite side of the body as the kicking leg.

Roundhouse Kick

From a back stance raise the back leg so that the foot is behind you, with the knee and the foot at the same level as the hips. At this point, the knee is bent and the inside of the leg is facing downward. The toes and the foot are extended and locked all the way back so that the instep will be striking the target. As the supporting foot and hips pivot forward, the kicking leg will swing forward until the knee is locked with the leg straight in front of the body, toes pointing straight out. Reverse the motion and return the leg into its cocked position and then set it down into a back stance. When the cane is used for support, it is most commonly on the opposite side of the body as the kicking leg.

Other kicks exist in American Eagle Cane Style such as heel kick, back kick, hook kick, and others, which are taught to higher ranking belts. These kicks are more complicated and are taught by an instructor in class.

CHAPTER 7
BASIC FORMS

BASIC FORMS
ADVANCED TECHNIQUES

BASIC FORMS

In the American Eagle Cane Style there are twenty-two basic forms. Basic forms are referring to the upper body movements or techniques of the cane most commonly done in forms or self-defense in this style. At the same time, these movements are to cover the range of basic knowledge in the style and give the students a tangible list of identified moves that will help them achieve success as they progress through their training.

1. Low Strike
2. Down Block
3. Center Block
4. High Block
5. Outside Block
6. Reinforced Down Block
7. Reinforced Center Block
8. Reinforced High Block
9. Overhead Strike
10. High Strike
11. Tip Strike
12. Lunge Strike
13. Vertical Punch
14. Double Punch (horn-up)
15. Low Parry Block
16. Reverse High Block
17. Low Crook Strike
18. Triple Crook Strike
19. Shaft Strike
20. Crook Punch
21. Forearm Block
22. Vertical Block

Understand that learning the 22 basic forms or basic techniques will give you the necessary foundation to reach a first degree black belt level of knowledge for American Eagle Cane Style. As a black belt your skills and abilities in mastering individual martial arts techniques will be truly challenged, for this style employs over 50 additional individual techniques. These vary from parry block, brace block, reverse brace block, reinforced outside block, high shaft block, horn strike, rotational block, accelerated blocks, and many more.

Also at this level the student should understand that visually and physically there is little difference between a block and a strike. The mental state of the user and the intent of the technique determine if it is a strike or a block, for a block can stop a physical conflict as easily as a strike. The difference arises in the intent. A block is intended to protect you from harm while a strike is intended to end the conflict.

The following pages cover the twenty-two basic forms for American Eagle Cane Style by description and illustration.

Moving in Basic Forms

You will step forward into the appropriate stance by moving the back foot for each technique. For example, if a down block were called, you would step your right foot forward into a right front stance and then execute the technique.

Basic forms are performed in groups of three, moving forward. For instance, you have "prepared for basic forms" and you are in a left front stance. You would perform three stances moving forward, each with a technique, as follows: right front stance, left front stance, and right front stance. On the completion of the third technique, kiyup, turn around, and transfer the cane to the other hand. For example, if the cane were in your right hand, once you have turned, it will now be in your left hand to repeat the process moving in the returning direction. When you change hands, the cane should be in the same grip as the previous technique and at an appropriate height. These subtleties will be covered by your instructor.

Prepare for Basic Forms

To begin basic forms you first go into a ready stance. From this position you step forward with your left leg into a left front stance. At the same time you swing the cane out from beneath your right arm from the crook grip and grasp it mid-shaft with your left hand, palm-up. Slide your right hand from the crook to the grip so that you are now holding the cane in a two-handed grip, with the tip at approximately the height of your sternum and the crook directed downward. Kiyup as you complete this movement.

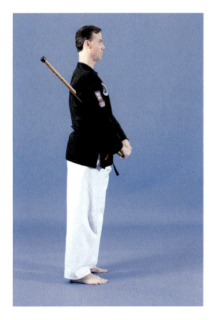

Turning Around in Basic Forms

On the completion of the third technique, you will turn around. The method of turning varies depending on the stance adopted, but all result in the rear leg becoming the new lead leg heading in the opposite direction.

For a **front stance**, slide the back foot over on the ball of the foot without losing contact with the ground so that it passes the lead leg by the same width to the opposite side as it started. Maintain the same length of the stance. Pivot on the balls of the feet to turn 180-degrees to face the opposite direction, and assume a proper front stance, as described in the section on stances.

For a **back stance**, pivot the lead foot 90-degrees and slide the back foot up so the heels of the two feet touch. At the same time, allow your body to turn to face 180-degrees in the opposite direction. The foot that has moved up will now become your lead leg. Slide it out to form a proper back stance, as described in the section on stances.

For a **horse stance**, no change is necessary to the feet. Look and turn the upper body to face 180-degrees in the opposite direction.

Basic Forms

The following basic forms will be described for the right hand holding the cane. Assume the other hand is a guard unless otherwise specified. These techniques should be practiced equally with the right and left sides of the body. Also assume a natural grip unless otherwise specified. The techniques described below are for the first ones executed after "prepare for basic forms," with the majority resulting in a lead leg; however, as you move for one stance to another, they may alternate between what is commonly identified as lead and reverse techniques. Therefore, execute the cane movements as described, but recognize that the stances may vary. In addition, they are described for the right hand only. See your instructor for clarification on these techniques for the left hand and other stances.

1. Low Strike

Raise the right hand, palm-up, near the right shoulder, bending at the elbow. Extend the arm at a downward angle, keeping the right palm-up, and tipping the wrist in order to maintain a straight line from the tip of the cane through the shaft and up the arm to the shoulder. The height of the tip from the floor should be approximately the same height of your own knee and in line with your lead leg.

2. Down Block

Keeping the right elbow close to the body, begin the motion of the technique by raising the cane to the outside of your body. Continue with your right hand passing by your right shoulder, in front of your body, and circling the cane downward to end with the right hand palm down. Tip the wrist in order to maintain a straight line from the tip of the cane through the shaft and up the arm to the shoulder. The height of the tip from the floor should be approximately the height of your own knee and in line with your lead leg. The crook points toward the right.

3. Center Block

Keeping the right elbow close to the body, begin the motion of the technique by raising the cane to the inside of your body. Continue with your right hand passing by your left shoulder, in front of your body, and circling the cane toward your right side to end with the right hand palm down. The crook is directed toward the floor. The shaft will be angled toward the right side, and with tip upwards. In executions of the center block, the shaft may end roughly parallel with the floor.

4. High Block

Raise your right hand overhead, rotating your wrist palm-away. Your right hand should end in line with your right shoulder joint with a bend in the elbow so that the shaft of the cane is approximately one-fist distance above the height of your head and one-fist distance to the front of the forehead. The wrist will be tipped slightly to allow the shaft to angle downward with the tip toward your left side. The crook points upward.

5. Outside Block

Keeping the right elbow close to the body, begin the motion of the technique by raising the cane to the outside of your body. The right hand will move upward toward the right with the tip directed upward so that the shaft begins to cross in front of your body before completing its downward motion. Continue with your right hand passing by your right shoulder, in front of your body, and circling the cane toward your left side to end with the right hand palm-down. The crook is directed toward the floor. The shaft will be angled across the front of your body toward the left and should end approximately parallel to the floor.

6. Reinforced Down Block

Keeping the right elbow close to the body, begin the motion of the technique by raising the cane to the outside of your body. Continue with your right hand passing by your right shoulder, in front of your body, and circling the cane downward. As the shaft passes by the head, your left hand leaves the guard hand position and the palm presses into the end-grip of the shaft. The circular motion of the cane now becomes linear, with both hands driving downward angle toward the front. The center of the shaft is centered with the body, and it is approximately one-fist distance above the lead leg. The crook points away and slightly downward. The shaft ends parallel with the floor, with the right hand palm down and the left hand open. The left wrist should be bent so that the fingers are tipped up and away from the cane. The shaft is positioned between the heel and center of the left palm.

7. Reinforced Center Block

Keeping the right elbow close to the body, begin the motion of the technique by raising the cane to the inside of your body. Continue with your right hand passing by your left shoulder, in front of your body, and circling the cane toward your right side. As the shaft passes by the left shoulder, your left hand leaves the guard hand position and the palm presses into the mid-grip. The technique ends with the tip upward and the shaft in line with the right hip. The crook is directed away from the body to the right. The right hand should be approximately the height of your right, lower ribs with the wrist tipped so the palm is behind the shaft of the cane. The palm of the left hand is on the cane's face with the striking edge facing to the right and the fingers not extending around the sides of the cane.

8. Reinforced High Block

Bend the right wrist to bring the shaft up in front of your body with the left hand leaving the guard hand position to press into the end-grip. Bend at the elbows to raise the cane up to chest height, parallel to the floor with the left wrist bent so the fingers point toward your body. Raise both hands to drive the shaft upward. Your right hand should end slightly wider than your right shoulder joint with a bend in the elbow. The shaft of the cane is approximately one-fist distance above the height of your head and one-fist distance to the front of the forehead. The crook points upward.

9. Overhead Strike

Raise your right hand to the right shoulder with the palm facing toward your head and the crook upwards. Extend the arm so the tip ends head height at the center of your body with the palm facing to the left and with a bend in the elbow.

10. High Strike

Raise your right hand to the right shoulder with the palm facing toward your head and the crook upwards. Extend the arm, bending the wrist, so the tip ends head height at the center of your body with the palm-up and with a bend in the elbow. The shaft is directed from right to left. The crook is directed to the left.

11. Tip Strike

Bring the right hand to the right hip (chamber) with the wrist bent so the shaft is level and the tip directed toward the center of your body. The crook is directed downward. The elbow remains behind the shaft of the cane throughout the technique, with the arm sliding lightly across the side of your body. Drive the tip forward to the height of the solar plexus. The arm maintains a slight bend to the elbow as the technique locks before drawing back with a slight recoil.

12. Lunge Strike

Grasp the mid-shaft, palm-up, with the left hand for a two-handed grip. Bring the right hand to the right hip (chamber) and the tip directed toward the center of your body with the left hand. The left hand arm will cross the front of your body with the forearm making light contact with your abdomen. The crook is directed downward. The right elbow remains behind the shaft of the cane throughout the technique. Drive the tip forward to the height of the solar plexus with both arms. The arms maintain a slight bend to the elbows as the technique locks before drawing back with a slight recoil.

13. Vertical Punch

Switch to a reverse mid-shaft grip. Bring the right hand back to the side of your ribs at mid-chest height with your fist vertical (palm facing inward). The elbow remains behind the shaft of the cane throughout the technique, with the arm sliding lightly across the side of your body. The crook faces to the rear near your right shoulder. Drive the right fist forward into the solar plexus keeping the shaft vertical. As you complete the punch draw the guard hand to the left chamber, creating a proper fist (palm-up).

14. Double Punch (horn-up)

Begin with a reverse crook grip, chambered on your right side. Execute two punches to the solar plexus, with the first punch completed with the right hand using the cane so that all four knuckles are used as the striking surface, and the second punch coming from the chamber as and empty-handed center punch. See the section on punches and guard hand techniques for further details. On the first punch, the guard hand will chamber.

15. Low Parry Block

Begin with a crook grip with the tip on the floor. Grasp the cane with the left hand near the grip. The right hand may remain on the top of the crook or slide slightly forward to where the crook first begins to bend. Pull with the right hand toward the opposite hip with the left hand assisting with the motion. The cane should remain vertical with the tip close to the floor through the technique. The parry motion is circular. If a low parry block has already been completed, and the right arm is across the body, then to execute another low parry, the right hand pulls toward the right side with the left hand assisting the motion.

16. Reverse High Block

   Raise your right hand overhead, rotating your wrist palm-toward your body. Your right hand should end in line with your left shoulder joint with a bend in the elbow so that the shaft of the cane is approximately one-fist distance above the height of your head and one-fist distance to the front of the forehead. The wrist will be tipped slightly to allow the shaft to angle downward with the tip toward your right side. The crook points upward. Your right arm will cross your body toward the left and your upper body will rotate slightly at the hips to bring the right shoulder forward.

17. Low Crook Strike

Begin with an end-grip, raise the right hand, palm-up, near the right shoulder, bending at the elbow. Extend the arm at a downward angle, keeping the right palm-up, and tipping the wrist in order to maintain a straight line from the end of the crook where it joins the shaft, through the shaft to the tip, and up the arm to the shoulder. The crook's height from the floor should be approximately the height your own knee and in line with your lead leg. The crook points toward the left. The strike is with the crook just above the horn. This strike may also use the shaft near the crook prior to a hooking technique.

18. Triple Crook Strike

Begin with an end-grip. Raise your right hand to the right shoulder (palm up) and execute a high strike with the crook directed to the left. Continue by bringing around overhead, turning it palm downward, and execute a high strike from left to right. Finally, bring the right hand straight back to the right shoulder (palm facing inward) and execute a downward strike. The crook strikes the same target three times. These are #5, #6, and #12 strikes.

19. Shaft Strike

Begin with a double-shaft grip. Bring the center of the shaft to the mid-chest, parallel to the floor with the elbows back and wrists tipped slightly so the palm is behind the shaft. Drive both hands forward, locking the elbows, so the shaft ends with the arms straight from the shoulders.

20. Crook Punch

Begin with the hand on the grip with the tip facing the floor and the crook facing forward. Tip the wrist so that the shaft is level and the crook is in the chamber directed downward. The elbow remains behind the shaft of the cane throughout the technique, with the arm sliding lightly across the side of your body. Drive the end of the crook forward to the height of the solar plexus. The arm maintains a slight bend to the elbow as the technique locks.

21. Forearm Block (Back Stance)

Begin with a double-shaft grip. Step into a back stance. Bring the left hand to the left chamber with the crook end pointing forward. Raise the right hand (palm away), driving the forearm upward so that it is centered above the head and approximately one-fist distance to the front. As the arm is raised, the cane is raised in unison, contributing to the power of the block, which is conducted by the arm. The cane does not block. The shaft of the cane is fairly vertical to the left side of the body with the crook up. On the next technique the process is repeated from the opposite side as a mirror image and will end tip up. This process alternates for each block.

22. Vertical Block

Begin with a double-shaft grip. Raise the left hand (palm away) so that it drives toward the right to end with the forearm parallel to the floor around shoulder height. The right hand rotates so the palm faces inward. The shaft ends vertically to the outside of the lead leg. The entire body contracts on completion of the technique. On the next move the processes is repeated ending crook up over to the opposite side. The process alternates for each block.

CHAPTER 8
SWINGS AND
MOVING TECHNIQUES

SWINGS
MOVING TECHNIQUES
12 STRIKES / 8 STRIKES
STRIKING TARGETS
THREE POINT SPARRING

SWINGS AND MOVING TECHNIQUES

Cane Swings

Cane swings refer to a variety of techniques where the cane is grasped in either a crook or reverse crook grip. From this grip, the cane is permitted to pivot within the palm so that the shaft completes a rotational motion. These motions can be vertical, horizontal, at an angle, or be directed to different heights. These techniques include side twirls, figure-eights (windmills), overhead twirls (helicopter twirls), and swing strikes. In addition, grips may be switched while various swing techniques are in motion in a method called reversing the horn (flipping the cane). These techniques are often used as transitional moves to the keep the cane in motion and the body in unison with the cane to prevent an interruption of flow. They may also be used as a defensive move to create space between the defender and attacker or as a barrier. However, all of these techniques are also effective as strikes; they are not just for aesthetic appeal or tournament flare.

A swing strike can generate tremendous speed and power through the shaft, and utilizes circular motion. A key aspect of control and safety for these techniques can be found in the subtlety of timing and total body control. Some of these elements include amount tension within the hand (especially the palm and fingers), flexion and extension of the wrist, movement at the elbow and shoulder, and hip rotation. In addition, placement of the hand at the start and endpoint of the technique will help to control how the shaft is accelerated and decelerated, preventing it from impacting the practitioner's own body with any substantial force. These elements should be learned under the direct supervision of a certified American Eagle Cane Style instructor. With all of this in mind, below are some of the swing techniques for this style.

Side Twirls

Begin with a crook grip. Turn the palm upward so the horn faces inward and the forearm is extended toward the front of your body. The forearm is somewhat parallel with the floor. Moving at the shoulder, elbow, and wrist, move the hand in a circular motion that is upward and forward then downward and backward. This will bring the shaft of the cane around in a complete circle in the direction coming from behind you as it rises and toward the floor in front of you as it descends. Keep the palm upward during this entire motion without turning the wrist over, and keep the elbow relatively close to the body.

Side twirls may begin with the tip on the floor; however, when first learning this technique, it may be helpful to position the tip upward with the crook resting in the palm of the hand. The grip must be loose enough to allow the crook to rotate, but closed so that the cane is always encircled by the fingers for control. Be aware that the tightly curved or narrow crooks can hook the wrist if this motion is not properly performed. Also, be aware of sharp horns as they will be rotating near your wrist.

This technique is commonly used to transition into a figure-eight, chambering, or reversing the crook, but it can also be extended as a strike. Side twirls are not commonly performed in the reverse direction because they are not as effective as a strike, do not permit flipping of the cane, do not permit quick chambering, and other considerations. Side twirls are not performed with a reverse crook grip with the palm down, although this motion is also possible to perform.

Chambering

Chambering refers to brining the shaft of the cane under the arm with the hand grasping the crook turning so the palm is facing inward. This can be performed from various grips and shaft positions. From a crook or reverse crook grip, the palm is turned downward to direct the shaft under the arm before it rotates to face inward. From a natural grip, the shaft is slid through the palm so that the hand is now on the crook, and the above procedure is followed. Chambering in this context refers to chambering the shaft, not the fist. Chambering the fist refers to bringing the hand next to hip, whether it is empty-handed or grasping a cane.

Figure-Eight

Figure-eights may be referred to as windmills. This technique may be visualized in a number of ways. Primarily, the motion of the shaft draws a number "8" which is turned on its side like an infinity symbol, ∞. The "X" portion of this symbol is where the cane is coming downward at an angle from right to left or from left to right. The loops on either side of the symbol are where the cane is arcing to change direction, passing by the sides of the body; whereas, the "X" occurs in front of the body.

A figure-eight may be performed from a crook or reverse crook grip. The other hand is in the guard hand position. The motion is also possible from a natural grip and others, but those advanced techniques will not be discussed in this textbook. This description is for the right hand on the crook, but the same process would be performed for the left hand as a mirror image.

Begin with the right hand near the right shoulder, loosely grasping the crook with the palm facing forward. The shaft lies along the back of the arm. Bring the right hand down at an angle in front of you toward the left side, palm down. As you do so, tip the wrist and allow the arm to move with the technique, keeping the elbow at approximately its natural height if you were standing with your arms at your side. As the shaft passes diagonally downward from right to left, raise the right hand toward the left shoulder and begin to turn your palm upward. This is considered one-half of the technique (sometimes referred to as half of a windmill or half of a figure eight). Continue by bringing the right hand down with the palm upward so the shaft descends at an angle from left to right. As it passes to your right side, raise the right hand toward the right shoulder and begin to turn the palm downward. At this point you have completed one entire figure-eight. You would be able to continue into another figure eight if you chose.

There are many subtleties to the movement of the body. In addition, the above description is for a full range of motion of the technique, but some of these movements can be shortened with the wrist doing more of the work. These aspects are best learned from your instructor.

Exchanging Hands

Exchanging hands refers to transferring the cane from the control of one hand to another by re-grasping it while in motion. This is most commonly done from a figure-eight. While executing the first "half" of a figure eight, your hand which is grasping the crook will descend in front of you palm down. Around this point, your guard hand will bring its palm to your closed fist which is encircling the cane. Both hands and arms continue the flow of the movement without pause, but in this short span of time, the hand opens to press the crook into the other hand, which receives it and closes (palm up) to continue into the second "half" of the figure-eight. The cane has exchanged hands. The importance is to always maintain contact with the cane and to not "throw" the cane from one hand to another.

It is noteworthy that there are advanced methods of exchanging the cane from hand to hand which are not discussed in this textbook. These allow for changing grips, can occur overhead or behind the back, and others.

Swing Strikes

Swings may be practiced with either a crook or reverse crook grip and you should practice both ways. The path of each strike travels from the tip on the floor through the intended target to your opposite hip. Learn to control the motion of the cane with pressure from your hand and the movement of your body rather than stopping the cane by allowing it to strike your body. Initially, it is easier to practice the swing strikes to a high target level, such as head high, and then move to lower targets. Practicing to different target heights will greatly increase your accuracy for swing strikes. Swing strikes may also be executed from a position with the shaft over the back of the arm or from a chambered position with a reverse crook grip. Remember to practice with both your right and left hands equally.

Overhead Twirls

Overhead twirls are sometimes referred to as helicopter twirls or techniques. They may be performed from a crook or reverse crook grip. Unlike swings and side twirls, the crook does not pivot in the hand, rather it is firmly gripped and the wrist is rotated to create the circular motion of the shaft. An overhead twirl is performed overhead with the shaft directed from the outside toward the inside of your body before continuing around behind you and should be overhead and roughly parallel to the floor.

In addition, a similar technique can be performed with the cane or walking staff (bo-cane) with the hands on the shaft. This technique is not covered in this textbook, but occurs in the kata Briar Patch.

Reversing the Horn

Reversing the horn is also called flipping the cane and refers to switching between a crook and reverse crook grip and *vice versa*. This is done while the cane is in motion from a side twirl, figure eight, or even an overhead twirl. There are a variety of ways to change the grip properly, but this method is the only one referred to as Reversing the Horn.

There are a variety of reasons to reverse the horn while in motion. For example, when the cane is chambered, horn down, in a crook grip, the cane cannot be horizontally swung from beneath arm due to the way the arm and wrist wrap the cane. However, when chambered, horn up, in a reverse crook grip, a horizontal swing is possible. Therefore, reversing the horn may be desired prior to chambering to allow for the possibility of a swing strike.

Reversing the Horn
(from a crook grip to a reverse crook grip)

The horn may be reversed on either side of the body. What is described here is flipping the cane on the outside of your body, as opposed to doing so with the arm across the body with the cane on the opposite side. Reversing the horn may occur from a variety of starting positions. What is described below is a method for beginners to practice until they become more familiar with the underlying fundamental motion.

Start with a crook grip with the tip facing upward, loosely gripping the cane. Turn the palm downward to initiate the rotational motion of the shaft in front of your body. Open the fingers so that the crook pivots around the thumb, and turn your palm upward to receive the cane. This motion should have the crook of the cane (or upper shaft) rotate around your hand so that the inside of the crook ends in the palm. Complete the motion by chambering. The cane should make one and one-half turns before the chambering and not simply be adjusted using the fingers or by dropping and catching the cane. See your instructor for clarification. Also consult your instructor regarding safety considerations when practicing this technique.

REVERSING THE HORN

Reversing the Horn
(from a reverse crook grip to a crook grip)

Reversing the horn back to a crook grip involves completing the flip with the arm across the body so that the cane is on the opposite side. Rotate the palm up to begin the circular motion of the cane at your side. Open the hand to re-grip in a manner similar to flipping the cane with it pivoting around your hand. See your instructor for the intricacies and subtleties of this technique.

MOVING CANE TECHNIQUES

The following are techniques often referred to as moving cane techniques. They can be done in a variety of stances moving from one end of a training hall to another. They may also be executed moving forwards or backwards; however, forwards is more common. There are additional moving cane techniques which would be considered *advanced techniques*, but they are not discussed in this textbook.

Swing Strikes

Figure-Eights

Overhead Twirls

Overhead Twirls to Swing Strike

8 Double-Handed Strikes (one strike per stance change)

12 Strikes (one strike per stance change)

STRIKING ANGLES

EIGHT DOUBLE-HANDED ANGLES

Starting with the cane held horizontally in front of you with a double shaft grip, the basic directions of the eight double-handed striking angles are as follows:

1. Horizontally, right to left

2. Horizontally, left to right

3. Diagonally upward, right to left

4. Diagonally downward, left to right

Note that an important shift in position happens between move #4 and move #5. Make sure you position yourself so that for strike #5 the left hand is lower than the right, and the primary striking happens with the end of the cane that is in your left hand. For move #6, the right hand is higher than the left, and the primary striking happens with the end of the cane that is in your right hand.

5. Straight upward- left end is primary striking end

6. Straight downward- right end is primary striking end

7. Diagonally upward, left to right

8. Diagonally downward, right to left

When you practice the eight double-handed striking angles from both sides, it is important to realize that the striking targets and possibilities for follow-up techniques are completely different depending upon if you hold the cane with the crook to the right and the tip to the left, or with the crook to the left and the tip to the right.

12 STRIKES

The 12 strikes are described here with the right hand. It is important to practice with both hands equally. When performed with the left hand, the 12 strikes will be a mirror image of those described below. Begin by practicing the 12 strikes from a natural stance. When directed by an instructor you will be stepping with each strike.

#1 Strike- Low strike to the ankle or knee on your right side (opponent's left side). Your hand will be palm up.

#2 Strike- Low strike to the opposite side of #1. Your hand will be palm down.

#3 Strike- Midlevel strike to hip or ribs on your right side (opponent's left side). Your hand will be palm up.

#4 Strike- Midlevel strike to the opposite side of #3. Your hand will be palm down.

#5 Strike- High strike to the side of the head on your right side (opponent's left side). Your hand will be palm-up up.

#6 Strike- High strike to the opposite side of #5. Your hand will be palm down.

#7 Strike- Angled strike down onto the collarbone on your right side (opponent's left side).

#8 Strike- Angled strike up into the low ribs on your left side (opponent's right side).

#9 Strike- Angled strike down onto the collarbone on your left side (opponent's right side).

#10 Strike- Angled strike up into the low ribs on your right side (opponent's left side)

#11 Strike- Striking straight upward. The cane will pass close to your body in a circular motion as you rotate your bod. The target area can be the groin, or if your opponent is leaning forward, it can be the midsection or the face. Note that the thumb side of your hand will be down for this strike.

#12 Strike- Striking straight downward onto the top of the head.

The 12 angled strikes may be practiced in a variety of ways:

Single-handed striking, as described above.

Double-handed striking. The opposite hand supports your lead hand from underneath, closer to the crook.

Single-handed striking with the crook, holding the end-grip.

Single-handed striking with the back of the crook, holding the end-grip.

Double-handed striking with the crook. The opposite hand supports your lead hand from underneath, closer to the tip.

Double-handed striking with the back of the crook. The opposite hand supports your lead hand from underneath, closer to the tip.

THREE POINT SPARRING

Three point sparring are partner drills that occur in sets of three predetermined attack and defense scenarios. These may occur with both partners using a cane, one partner using a cane and the other being empty-handed, or both partners being empty-handed. Below you will find just two examples of three-point sparring practiced in the American Eagle Cane Style.

CANE VS. CANE

Attacker:

1. Step forward into a RFS and execute a #5 strike

2. Step forward into a LFS and execute a #6 strike

3. Step forward into a RFS and execute a #12 strike

Defender:

1. Step right foot back into a LFS and execute a reinforced outside block

2. Step back into a RFS and execute a reinforced parry block

3. Step back into a LFS and execute a reinforced high block, then

Counter with a redirection of the attacker's cane to your right followed by a lunge strike to the face.

EMPTY-HAND VS. CANE

<u>Attacker (empty handed)</u>

1. Step forward into a RFS and execute a right high punch

2. Step forward into a LFS and execute a left high punch

3. Step forward into a RFS and execute a right high punch

<u>Defender (cane in a double-shaft grip)</u>

1. Step the right foot back into a LFS and execute a high shaft block

2. Step back into a RFS and execute a diagonal shaft block (crook up)

3. Step back into a LFS and execute a diagonal shaft block (tip up), then

Counter with a crook strike to the solar plexus.

Transition: After the counter has been completed, the empty-handed attacker transitions into the cane-holding defender by grasping the cane with their right hand (palm down) at the grip, rotates their right hand to palm-up, grasps the end-grip with the left hand (palm down), and opens the right hand to shift the grip to palm-down.

Striking Points

Freeing oneself up from a grab does not necessarily free you up from a dangerous situation. Finding yourself in this position may result in you having to take more definite action. The following diagram indicates seven of the best areas to strike while defending yourself. The most effective striking area is the knee. The effectiveness of striking these areas will depend on: the technique used, the amount of power projected on point of impact, and the type of clothes, including shoes, that are being worn by the attacker.

1) Eyes **2)** Cervical Vertebrae **3)** Clavicle **4)** Elbow **5)** Solar Plexus **6)** Groin **7)** Knee

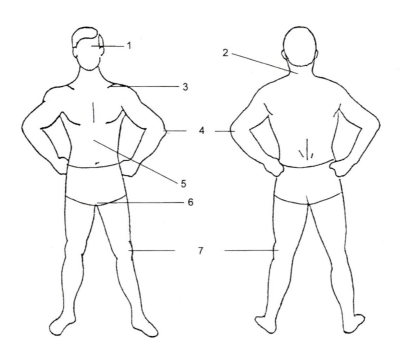

In addition the cane can be used effectively to strike additional areas such as the instep, shin, upper thigh, hip, coccyx, thoracic or lumbar vertebrae, sternum, radius, ulna, hand, and throat. Different parts of the cane will result in different effects.

The theme of self-defense in the American Eagle Cane Style is first to make sure that you do not get hurt and to not focus effort on hurting the person attacking you. As you defend yourself, the end result may be that the attacker does get hurt, but it should be looked upon only as a side effect of you freeing yourself from a dangerous and possibly life-threatening situation.

CHAPTER 9
SELF-DEFENSE

INTRODUCTION TO SELF-DEFENSE
CTS 1-75
ADVANCED SELF-DEFENSE

American Eagle Cane Style

Self Defense

This style of martial arts offers a unique combination of Korean, Japanese and Chinese traits that, when combined with each other and added to American self-defense styles, bring about a powerful form of training and skill. As you read and study this instructional workbook you will see the tradition of the martial arts attitude maintained with its courtesy and respect for all styles, and the enthusiastic pride of our style.

The American Eagle Cane Style of self-defense is greatly focused on a concept of scissors motions and leverage exerted by the cane. Strikes and kicks can take place at any time during the flow, yet the purpose is normally to lock up and take control of the attacker. Once in control, the choice for injury is up to the attacker. In short, if they stop moving and/or fighting, they will not be hurt, but to continue the assault once a joint is neutralized is to bring about injury. Because of this structure, many of these moves look soft and gentle which allows them to be done in a crowded area without onlookers feeling that you are becoming too aggressive and brutal.

Please keep in mind that to do self-defense techniques well you need an instructor that is working with you. That instructor is taking into account your height, weight, strength and level of self-confidence as they teach you defensive moves that will work for you. A good technique does not mean it is good for everyone or every situation.

Also realize that you do not need a hundred techniques, sixty techniques or even twenty techniques to defend yourself. There are only so many ways that you can be grabbed and to have one technique you like and know well to counter a grab is all you really need on the street. Most individuals go through their whole life and are never attacked. However, certain individuals work in areas or occupations that result in their becoming involved in physical conflict regularly. Others may live in a high-risk area or give off the signals that they are a target and are sometimes attacked more than once in their lifetime.

The primary ways you are attacked or grabbed:

(These are not in any specific order and exclude weapons such as knives, guns, clubs, chains, etc.)

Grabs:

Hair grab from behind or in front

Bear hug from behind or in front

Cross wrist grab

Straight across wrist grab

Throat grab (one hand or two hands)

Lapel grab (single or double)

Shoulder grab

Sleeve grab

Rear chokehold

Attacks:

Punch to the face

Punch to the solar plexus

Punch to the side of the rib cage

Kick to the face

Kick to the solar plexus

Kick to the groin

Kick to the knee

Kick to the side of the rib cage

Cane strike or lunge to the head

Cane strike or lunge to the solar plexus

Cane strike or lunge to ribs

Cane strike or lunge to knee

NOTE: the term "Cane Strike" can refer to any rigid striking implement including a pipe, stick, or other similar device.

The self-defense that is used here has one major difference than that which is used in our personal safety programs. The difference here is the choice to take control of the aggressive actions that are being forced on you. In our personal safety programs, our main aim is to escape the situation and seek additional assistance.

Safety

Safety is the most important aspect when practicing self-defense. Keep in mind that when practicing self-defense with another student, they are not your opponent, but your partner who is helping you to learn. Their safety is your responsibility and should be an absolute priority during training. Go slowly when learning self-defense techniques. Quality of movement and understanding the techniques are more important than going fast.

Always make sure you are using a cane that is appropriate for self-defense practice. Never use a cane with very aggressive features, especially one with a sharpened horn, when working with a partner. Use extra caution for joint locks or when the crook is around your partner's neck. In addition, the partner who is having the technique applied to them should be in good communication with their practice partner by "tapping out" to indicate when appropriate pressure is felt or to indicate that the technique is "working."

It is essential that you review the safety points for each technique noted in this section or explained to you by your instructor. Some of the techniques end with a throw or a takedown for use in real self-defense applications. For these techniques, do not throw your training partner unless under the direct supervision of an instructor who has indicated that you may do so. During practice, students will generally complete the technique up until the point where their partner is unbalanced, but they do not complete the throw. Some takedowns may be allowed in certain situations, with safety mats and under close supervision of a certified instructor. Keep in mind that even when both partners are being very careful it may be hard to anticipate unexpected events. If your partner should accidentally start to fall during a self-defense technique that involves a joint lock or with the crook around the neck, release the lock or let go of your cane. Safety for your partner, yourself, and the people around you is your responsibility when it comes to the control of your cane.

CTs: Cane Techniques

The CTs (Cane Techniques) are fundamental self-defense exercises which may be practiced both with and without a partner. When practiced without a partner, you should seek to execute them with precision of formal stances and a full range of body motion through the techniques. When practiced with a partner, the techniques will need to be executed with the safety of your partner in mind. In addition, the stances will need to be altered so that the lower body foundation is correct for the technique but is adapted to the partner's body position, height, *et cetera*. These considerations will need to be learned under the supervision of a qualified and certified instructor. It is also important to understand that the CTs, as described below, are not step-by-step mechanical motions as the directions might seem to imply. The directions are meant to provide enough specificity to allow you to review and practice once you have been taught the technique, but they lack the subtlety, body flow, changes of tension and power, timing, distance considerations, and other aspects which are essential.

It is extremely important to keep in mind that the directions provided for these CTs are for the right hand only. Learn, and become comfortable with, each CT with the cane in the right hand first. The directions will be reversed when you practice the cane in the left hand.

CT-1
Attack: Right Punch
Chambered Reverse Crook Grip

1. Step forward into LFS: execute a left knife hand.

2. Execute a right punch to the solar plexus with the crook end. Simultaneously, chamber the left hand.

CT-2

Attack: Right Punch

Cane Held: Natural Grip

1. Step forward into LFS: execute a center block to the outside of the attacker's right arm. Left guard hand.

2. Step forward past the attacker's right side: execute a low strike to the attacker's right knee.

3. Step the left foot around clockwise 180⁰ to face the attacker's back. Bring the cane between you and the attacker and execute an overhead strike to the attacker's head from behind with the cane coming up from your left side.

Safety: do not make contact to the shin or head.

CT-3

Attack: Double-Lapel Grab
Cane Held: Natural Grip

1. Bring shaft from the right and over the attacker's forearms so the tip end points to the left.

2. Grab the shaft with the left hand (palm down) near the outside of the attacker's left arm.

Note: the shaft may lie anywhere from the elbow joint to the wrist joint, but most often done mid-forearm

3. Pull downward on the shaft, drawing it in toward the center of your body.

4. Execute a shaft strike to the attacker's head.

Safety: do not make contact with the face or throat.

CT-4
Attack: Right Punch
Cane Held: Natural Grip

1. Step forward into LFS: execute a center block to the outside of the attacker's right arm. Left guard hand.

2. Switch the grip on the cane by bringing the shaft down to the right then up to your left hand and grasp the end-grip (palm down), release the right hand and re-grasp the shaft (palm up) next to your left hand (closer to the crook end). Simultaneously, step right foot forward past the attacker's right side. Execute a low strike with the shaft (crook facing forward) into the attacker' right shin.

3. Step left foot around clockwise 180⁰ so you are facing the attacker's back. Pull on the cane to hook the attacker's right ankle with the crook, and rotate your wrists and forearms so the crook rotates toward the floor to lock on to the attacker's ankle. This would allow you to pull for a takedown.

Safety: do not strike the shin or pull on the ankle.

CT-5

Attack: Right Punch

Cane Held: Natural Grip

1. Step forward into a LFS: execute a left knife hand block to the inside of the attacker's right forearm.

2. Bring the shaft up so that the tip of the cane ends between the attacker's legs, toward their back. Note: this could be a strike but it is not necessary.

3. Rotate the right hand (palm up), so the shaft lies across the front of that attacker's right thigh and the tip lies behind the attacker's left knee or upper hamstring.

4. Step right foot forward past the attacker's right side. Simultaneously, push right hand forward to apply pressure on the attacker's right thigh. Note: keep the cane to the front of your body entire time, and direct the shaft of the cane forward but parallel to the floor.

Safety: do not complete a takedown; maintain safety for their knees and ankles.

CT-6

Attack: Left Punch

Cane Held: Double-Shaft Grip

1. Step forward into a LFS: execute a vertical block to the inside of the attacker's left arm (tip up).

2. Slide the cane forward and up so that the tip end extends beyond the attacker's neck from their left side, and rotate your right wrist so the crook turns upward to hook around the attacker's left wrist or forearm.

3. Pull down on the shaft of the cane with the left hand toward the left hip while raising the right hand (so the crook end is high).

CT-7

Attack: Bear Hug

Cane Held: Reverse Crook Grip

1. Bring the crook over the attacker's hands or wrists facing your body. Grip the cane with the left hand above the right. Pull straight down to release the attacker's grip.

2. Step left foot forward (away from attacker). Slide the right hand down to mid-shaft, and execute a tip strike backwards to the attacker's solar plexus from your right side.

3. Rotate your body at the waist clockwise and bring the cane shaft to the left side of the attacker's head. Complete by rotating at the waist counterclockwise to execute a strike with the shaft to the left side of the attacker's head.

CT-8

Attack: Right Punch

Cane Held: Chambered Reverse Crook Grip

1. Step forward into a LFS: execute a left knife hand block to the inside of the attacker's right forearm.

2. Execute a right punch to the attacker's right upper thigh (quadriceps muscles).

CT-9

Attack: Right Punch

Cane Held: Chambered Reverse Crook Grip

1. Step forward into a LFS: execute a left knife hand block to the inside of the attacker's right forearm.

2. Extend the right arm forward and beyond the left side of the attacker's neck, rotating the wrist palm down so the crook is prepared to hook the neck from behind. Simultaneously, chamber the left hand as a fist.

3. Pull the right hand down toward the center of your chest (pulling the attacker's head down with the crook or horn) and execute a left forearm strike to the right side of the attacker's head (left fist is palm down).

CT-10

Attack: Right Punch

Cane Held: Natural Grip

1. Step forward into a LFS: execute a center block to the outside of the attacker's right arm. Left guard hand.

2. Grasp the end-grip with the left hand (palm away), and push the shaft down toward your right (to move the arm).

3. Step right foot forward past the attacker's right side, and hook the attacker's neck with the crook. Simultaneously, switch the right hand from a palm down grip to a palm up grip.

4. Step the left foot around clockwise so you are behind the attacker and turned perpendicular to the right. Slide the right hand up the shaft toward the crook so your right fist is tight to the back of the attacker's neck and your forearm is along the attacker's spine (elbow below fist). Your left hand grasps near the end-grip.

Safety: exercise caution around the neck.

CT-11

Attack: Right Punch

Cane Held: Mid-Shaft Grip

1. Step forward into a LFS: execute a center block to the outside of the attacker's right arm (crook up). Left guard hand.

2. Step right foot forward past the attacker's right side, and hook the attacker's neck with the crook. Grasp the end grip palm down with the left hand

3. Step the left foot around clockwise so you are behind the attacker and turned perpendicular to the right. Slide the right hand up the shaft toward the crook so your right fist is tight to the back of the attacker's neck and your forearm is along the attacker's spine (elbow below fist). Your left hand grasps the end-grip, palm down.

Safety: exercise caution around the neck.

CT-12

Attack: Left Punch

Cane Held: Natural Grip

1. Step forward into a LFS: execute a center block to the inside of the attacker's left arm.

2. Grasp the end grip with the left hand (palm away), and execute a crook strike to the attacker's left floating ribs by bringing the left hand (tip end) to the left hip and the right hand (crook end) across horizontally.

CT-13

Attack: Right Kick

Cane Held: Natural Grip

1. Step left foot to the left into a back stance to avoid kick.

2. Execute a center block downward on top of the attacker's right shin.

CT-14

Attack: Right Kick

Cane Held: Natural Grip

1. Step right foot to the right into a back stance to avoid kick.

2. Execute an outside block downward on top of the attacker's right shin.

CT-15

Attack: Right Kick

Cane Held: Natural Grip

1. Step right foot back into a LFS: execute a low block to the inside of the attacker's right leg.

2. Execute a vertical strike to the attacker's groin.

CT-16

Attack: Left Sleeve Grab from Side

Cane Held: Natural Grip

1. Bring the cane up and grab the shaft with the left hand (palm down) near the mid-shaft or tip end.

2. Step left foot to the left (toward the attacker). Execute a tip strike to the attacker's right floating ribs.

3. Bring cane shaft to the front of the attacker's right arm but behind the attacker's head, and execute a strike with the shaft to the back of the attacker's head (or the back of the neck for a takedown).

CT-17

Attack: Left Sleeve Grab from Side

Cane Held: Natural Grip

1. Bring the cane up and grab the shaft with the left hand (palm down) near the mid-shaft or tip end.

2. Step left foot to the left (toward the attacker). Execute a tip strike to the attacker's right floating ribs.

3. Bring cane shaft to the back of the attacker's right arm near the elbow. Complete by striking through to the front to break the attacker's grip. Note: bring your right arm through to the right hip as you follow through.

CT-18

Attack: Bear Hug

Cane Held: Mid-Shaft Grip

1. Allow cane to slide through right hand into a grip closer to the tip end of the shaft. Swing the right arm up and back, rotating the wrist so the shaft of the cane strikes into the attacker's neck from behind and the crook faces to the front. You can rotate at the waist and turn the right shoulder to the right.

2. Pull the cane toward the right, allowing the shaft to slide across the neck to hook the crook around the attacker's neck.

3. Grasp the end grip with the left hand. You can slide the right hand back at this point.

4. Step right foot forward and bring cane shaft down toward your left hip and the right hand straight over your right shoulder toward the ground.

Safety: do not throw your partner.

CT-19

Attack: Cross wrist grab to hand on cane

Cane Held: Crook Grip

1. Slide right hand down to a natural grip.

Note: the attacker's hand will still be on your hand.

2. Rotate right wrist palm up to bring the shaft of the cane up between you and the attacker and over so that it lies across the attacker's wrist.

3. Reach left hand up from underneath to grab the shaft of the cane palm up to the right of your right hand. The left forearm should lie along the shaft of the cane and trap the attacker's wrist from below.

4. Step back with the right foot and pull down on the cane toward your lower abdomen and tip your wrists away from you.

157

CT-20

Attack: Straight-across Right Sleeve Grab

Cane Held: Natural Grip

1. Reach across with your left hand and grab the attacker's left hand or wrist (palm towards you) to lock it to your upper arm, creating a fixed point.

2. Bring the shaft of the cane up from the right, outside the attacker's left arm, and lay it over the attacker's left arm and across their neck so the tip end lies on the attacker's right neck.

3. Bring the right hand (and crook end) under the attacker's left arm across to the left to apply leverage to the attacker's head and left elbow joint.

CT-21

Attack: Right Punch

Cane Held: Natural Grip

1. Step left foot forward into a LFS: execute a left knife hand block to the inside of the attacker's right forearm. Execute a vertical strike with the shaft to just above the attacker's right elbow.

2. Tip the right wrist so the shaft angles back to meet your open left hand, and grasp the shaft at this point.

3. Continue by bringing your left arm forward and the right hand (holding the shaft) back to trap the attacker's right forearm between your left forearm and the shaft, while stepping with your right foot.

4. Step with your left foot to rotate your body toward the attacker and take control of the shoulder joint.

CT-22

Attack: Right Punch

Cane Held: Natural Grip

1. Step left foot forward into a LFS: execute a left knife hand block to the inside of the attacker's right forearm followed by a grab to the attacker's right wrist.

2. Execute a vertical strike with the shaft to just above the attacker's right elbow.

3. Raise your right hand slightly forward and upward, tipping your right wrist to direct the shaft to lie across the front of the attacker's neck.

4. Step the right foot forward past the attacker's right side. Simultaneously, raise the attacker's right arm up to create a bend in the elbow. Continue by bringing the arm over and downward while pulling on the shaft to the right.

Safety: be aware that this technique can result in a takedown.

CT-23

Attack: Right Throat Grab

Cane Held: Double-Shaft Grip

1. Execute a vertical block (crook up) to the inside of the forearm.

2. Continue by rotating the shaft so the tip is high to redirect the arm to your right on the outside of their arm.

3. Extend the shaft at the tip end to the left side of the attacker's neck, and pull downward to the left hip for a takedown.

CT-24

Attack: Left Punch

Cane Held: Natural Grip

1. Execute a left palm check to the inside of the attacker's left forearm to redirect the arm so it lies next to the right side of your neck.

2. Bring the shaft up to the outside of the attacker's left triceps (tip up).

3. Step forward slightly with the right foot: Grasp the shaft of the cane with your left hand above the attacker's arm (palm away).

4. Using shaft pressure, roll the attacker's triceps over to rotate the attacker's arm so their elbow is toward the ceiling. The shaft now lies across the back of the attacker's upper arm and their left wrist is on your right shoulder.

5. Press downward.

CT-25

Attack: Sleeve Grab (arm holding cane)

Cane Held: Natural Grip

1. Bring the shaft from the right and over the attacker's arm so the tip end points to the left.

2. Grab the shaft with the left hand (palm down) near the attacker's left arm.

3. Pull downward on the shaft, drawing it in toward the center of your body. The best position for the cane is with the right hand very close to the attacker's right elbow joint.

4. Step the left foot back to outside of attacker. Raise your right hand (crook end) so the shaft presses up from underneath the attacker's right triceps and bring the left hand down in front of your body so the shaft presses down on top of the attacker's left forearm.

Safety: exercise caution with your partner's shoulder joint.

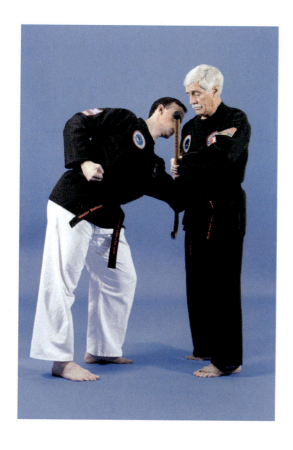 

CT-26

Attack: Grab Hand on Cane (from right side)

Cane Held: Seated: Crook Grip

1. Grab the attacker's hand (palm down) with your left hand, locking the attacker's left hand down onto your right hand and the crook of the cane.

2. Raise your right elbow up between you and the attacker and then bring it forward over the attacker's left wrist and lower forearm so that your right forearm lies on top of the attacker's left arm and to the front of your bodies. Note: This will bend your right wrist which is holding firmly on the crook.

3. Bring your forearm down and backwards, applying pressure to the attacker's left forearm and wrist.

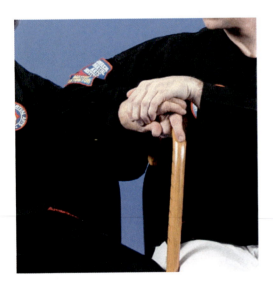

CT-27

Attack: Left Kick

Cane Held: Mid-Shaft Grip

The cane is normally held in a mid-shaft grip but quickly shifts to an end-grip.

1. Step into a RFS: execute a low block to the outside of the attacker's lower left leg. This shifts the attacker's body to the right, turning the front of their body away.

2. Execute a vertical strike upward to the attacker's groin with the back of the shaft near the crook. The shaft is between the attacker's legs and the crook extends beyond the attacker to the front of their body.

3. Rotate your wrist to hook the upper thigh, and pull the shaft backward. Your guard hand is prepared to press into the attacker's upper back to execute a takedown or strike.

CT-28

Attack: Right Shoulder Grab from Behind

Cane Held: Natural Grip

1. Bring the shaft up to your left hand, and grasp it in a double-shaft grip.

2. Rotate clockwise, stepping the right foot around between you and the attacker. Execute a vertical block to the outside of the attacker's right arm (at the elbow) by raising the left hand (tip up) and following across to the right side.

3. Execute a high crook strike to the attacker's left jaw.

CT-29

Attack: Bear Hug

Cane Held: Mid-Shaft Grip

1. Bring the tip of the cane up in front of you, and grasp the end-grip with the left hand while switching the right hand grip. Step left foot to left into a horse stance. Execute a crook strike down onto the top arc of the attacker's left foot. Keep hips close to the attacker and drop your center of gravity by bending the knees.

2. Hook the crook around the attacker's left ankle. The crook may point either direction.

3. Pull forward and up on the shaft while shifting your hips into the attacker by "sitting" down onto the attacker's thigh.

CT-30

Attack: Upper Cane Shaft Grabbed from Side

Cane Held: Crook Grip

1. Grasp the cane mid-shaft with your left hand (palm up).

2. Use the attacker's hand as a pivot point and strike with the opposite end of the shaft into the attacker's lower shin then up to the attacker's face.

CT-31

Attack: Cane Grabbed with two hands
Cane Held: Natural Grip

1. Grasp the shaft with your left hand (palm down) near the attacker's hands (LFS)

2. Step forward with the right foot: Bring the crook end of the cane up from your right, shifting the right hand by opening it and sliding it under the shaft near the crook with an open palm.

3. Complete the motion by pressing the right palm forward into the shaft of the cane to drive it into the attacker's face.

Safety: exercise caution not to make contact with your partner's face.

CT-32

Attack: Cane Grabbed with two hands

Cane Held: Natural Grip

1. Close the guard hand into a fist (in preparation for an empty-hand down block).

2. Step back into a LBS: execute a down block with your left arm so that it impacts into the attacker's wrists. Simultaneously, pull the shaft back toward your right shoulder.

3. Execute a high strike to the left side of the head.

CT-33

Attack: Cross Wrist Grab

Cane Held: Reverse Crook Grip

1. Your left wrist has been grabbed. Keep your left elbow low, bring the hand up toward the right, rotate your wrist and grab the attacker's left wrist with your left hand. Simultaneously, "pop" the cane up in the right hand from a reverse crook grip to a mid-shaft grip (crook up).

2. Pull the attacker's left wrist toward your left hip. Step the right foot forward and press down on the elbow with the shaft. Your right foot should be beneath the attacker's left elbow.

CT-34

Attack: Single Lapel Grab

Cane Held: Mid-Shaft Grip

1. Bring the crook under the attacker's right arm and then up to hook the crook over the attacker's right wrist so the crook points to the right from the outside.

2. Bring your left hand up so your left forearm is under both the attacker's right wrist and the shaft, and grab the end of the crook palm-down, trapping the attacker's right wrist between your wrist and the crook area.

3. Pull your left hand down toward the center of your lower abdomen, applying leverage with the crook on the attacker's wrist.

CT-35

Attack: Right Punch

Cane Held: Natural Grip

1. Step forward into a LFS: execute a left knife hand block to the inside of the attacker's right arm and a outside block to the attacker's biceps muscle.

2. Bring your left hand under the attacker's right arm, bringing the attacker's arm over your left shoulder. Simultaneously, raise your right hand so the shaft rolls to the outside of the attacker's right arm with the tip down and the crook up. Grab the shaft with your left hand (palm down) below, but close to, the attacker's right arm.

3. Press the shaft toward your right, then slightly upward (lifting the triceps muscle), and complete by rotating the shaft clockwise so that it ends parallel to the floor. The attacker's elbow ends pointing up to the ceiling so the arm is locked. Press straight down toward the floor.

CT-36

Attack: Left Punch

Cane Held: Mid-Shaft Grip

1. Execute a center block (crook up) to the inside of the attacker's left forearm.

2. Continue circular motion of the block to the outside of attacker's body, clearing the attacker's left arm away and striking with shaft to the outside of the attacker's left knee with the crook pointed to the left.

3. Step left foot forward (to inside of attacker's stance) and execute a left arc hand to the attacker's throat, turning your body so the left shoulder leads. Simultaneously, pull cane shaft back toward right hip.

Note: the cane crook has hooked the attacker's left knee from behind.

CT-37

Attack: Left Punch
Cane Held: Mid-Shaft Grip

1. Execute a center block (crook up) to the inside of attacker's left forearm.

2. Strike the attacker's jaw with the end of the crook.

3. Slide the crook past the left side of the attacker's neck and hook the neck from behind.

4. Pull down on the shaft, step the left foot across to the left (passing the right side of the attacker), and drive the lower end of the shaft into the groin.

5. Step with the right foot, then the left foot around behind the attacker and grab the end of the shaft with the left hand (palm down), releasing the right hand. Pull up on the shaft of the cane.

Safety: do not allow partner to roll forward.

CT-38

Attack: Right Punch

Cane Held: Natural Grip

1. Step forward into a RFS: execute a left knife hand block to the inside of the attacker's right forearm and an outside block to the attacker's right arm, simultaneously.

2. Grasp the end-grip of the shaft with the left hand (palm down), step the right foot CCW perpendicular in front of the attacker, and hook the crook around the left side of the attacker's neck.

3. Step right foot CCW in front of the attacker, so your back is facing the attacker and your hips are close. Your right elbow should be high. Complete with a CCW step back with the left foot.

Safety: While this technique is completed by executing a throw, do not actually throw your partner complete the throw.

CT-39

Attack: Right Punch

Cane Held: Natural Grip

1. Step left foot forward into a LFS: execute a reverse parry block to the outside of the attacker's right forearm.

2. Raise the tip so the shaft impacts the right side of the attacker's neck (crook facing left).

3. Step the right foot forward past the attacker and to the right so your hips are behind the attacker's hips, and slide the shaft forward so the crook hooks around the front of the attacker's throat. Keep the elbow of the right arm high.

4. Grasp the shaft with your left hand (palm down).

5. Pull down with right hand and execute throw.

Safety: do not actually throw your partner.

CT-40

Attack: Right Punch

Cane Held: Natural Grip

1. Step left foot forward to the left (moving to attacker's right side): execute a center block to the right arm.

2. Step the right foot forward past the attacker: execute a low strike to the middle of the attacker's shins so the tip protrudes beyond the attacker's left leg.

3. Step the left leg around CW, turning into the attacker and bending at the knees (so your shoulders are below the attacker's hips), and grasp the end-grip with the left hand (palm down).

4. Pull equally with both hands applying pressure on the shins with the shaft, while pushing upward and forward with your right shoulder into the attacker's upper leg, driving them forward.

5. As the attacker falls forward, continue the motion of the shaft by now pushing forward down onto the attacker's shins.

CT-41

Attack: Right Punch

Cane Held: Natural Grip

1. Step left foot forward into a LFS: execute a center block to the right arm.

2. Slide the shaft forward across the front of the attacker's throat until your right hand is close to the right side of the attacker's neck.

3. Grasp the shaft of the cane with the left hand (palm down) near the left side of the attacker's neck by reaching from behind the attacker.

4. Pull the shaft down toward your chest at an angle, pushing your chest forward to exert pressure and trap the attacker by the neck.

5. Step the right foot between you and the attacker: execute throw by rotating at the hips and bringing the attacker around by their head using the pressure of the cane.

<u>Safety</u>: do not actually complete the throw

179

CT-42

Attack: Left Punch

Cane Held: Natural Grip

1. Step forward into a RFS: execute a left knife hand block to the outside of the attacker's left forearm. Allow the cane to lag so that it remains positioned between you and the attacker.

2. Grab the attacker's left wrist with your left hand, and execute a #4 strike to the attacker's solar plexus.

3. With the shaft positioned against the attacker's abdomen, rotate the right hand to palm up without changing the grip. Simultaneously, bring the attacker's left arm toward your right hip to interweave the cane from under the attacker's body to over the triceps region of the attacker's left arm.

4. Step right foot toward the left, into the attacker, and press the right hand down to apply leverage of the shaft on the upper left arm of the attacker.

CT-43

Attack: Left Punch

Cane Held: Natural Grip

1. Step the right foot forward to the right: execute a knife hand block with your left hand to the outside of the attacker's left wrist.

2. Strike up to the right side of the attacker's neck with the shaft by bringing the cane from below the attacker's left arm with your right hand grip rotated palm up.

3. Reach your left arm across the left side of the attacker's neck and grab the shaft palm away near the attacker's neck.

4. Pull with both hands down toward your chest, allowing the left forearm to pressing forward into the attacker's neck (sometimes referred to as a scissor's hold or lock).

CT-44

Attack: Left Punch

Cane Held: Natural Grip

This series of movements rely on natural fluid movement, the direction of the arm, and interweaving of the cane.

1. Execute a palm check with the left hand to the inside of the attacker's left forearm, and step forward into a RFS:. Quickly follow these motions of redirection by hooking the crook over the attacker's wrist from the inside and over the top (crook points to the right). The right hand's grip is firm and rotated so the palm faces to the right and the elbow is high.

2. Lower the right arm's elbow and rotate the wrist so the shaft rises from beneath the attacker's left arm and begins to bend their arm at the elbow joint. The attacker's left wrist is lowered toward their left hip. The shaft of the cane should lie along the shoulder joint.

3. In flow, step the left foot forward and grab the shaft of the cane near the mid-shaft (palm down).

4. Rotate your hips and body CCW into the attacker and in flow, direct the crook end of the cane up toward the attacker's back while pressing down on the shaft at the shoulder joint.

CT-45

Attack: Right Punch

Cane Held: Natural Grip

1. Step forward into a LFS: execute a left knife hand block to the inside of the attacker's right arm.

2. Grab the attacker's right wrist with your left hand, and execute a vertical strike with the shaft up into the attacker's right triceps or armpit.

3. Pull the attacker's right arm down straight toward left hip. Simultaneously, raise the crook up and away at an angle so the shaft presses into the attacker's lower back and your right hand grip is rotated so the palm is upward.

4. Step the right foot past the attacker's right side. Drive your right hand away and down toward the floor to complete a takedown. The pressure of the shaft lies along the attacker's upper humerus and lumbar vertebrae.

CT-46

Attack: Right Punch

Cane Held: Mid-Shaft Grip

1. Simultaneously, execute a left knife hand block to the inside of the attacker's right forearm and an outside block (crook up) into the inside of the attacker's upper right arm.

2. Rotate the right wrist so the crook points toward the right. Strike the shaft near the crook into the right side of the attacker's neck.

3. Pull downward to hook the attacker's neck.

4. Step the left foot forward and toward the right, rotating your body clockwise so your hips are perpendicular to the attacker's hips and your feet are positioned within their stance. Simultaneously, grasp the shaft of the cane with the left hand (palm down) with the elbow high so the forearm presses into the right side of the attacker's neck.

5. Execute throw.

Safety: do not actually throw your partner.

184

CT-47
Attack: Right Punch
Cane Held: Mid-Shaft Grip

1. Step forward into a LFS: execute a center block to the outside of the attacker's right arm (crook up). Continue the motion of the shaft toward the right so the cane lies on top of the attacker's right arm and directs their punch downward.

2. Step right foot forward and continue motion of cane by extending the cane past the left side of the attacker's neck, rotate the wrist and direct the cane so the shaft lies along the back of the attacker's neck. The crook points to the left and away from you.

3. Interweave the left arm from under the shaft on the right side of the attacker's neck, bending at the elbow and bringing the left hand under the attacker's chin.

4. Press the left hand up and away, while pulling the right hand back.

Safety: this creates a great deal of pressure on the partner's cervical vertebrae. Exercise great caution

CT-48

Attack: Right Punch

Cane Held: Reverse Crook Grip

1. Step forward into a LFS: execute a left knife hand block to the inside of the attacker's right forearm. "Pop" the cane up into a mid-shaft grip, and execute a strike with the end of the crook to the solar plexus.

2. Hook the attacker's lead leg (from the outside of the leg, crook facing in). Execute a left arc hand to the attacker's throat.

3. Simultaneously, pull the shaft back to the right hip.

CT-49

Attack: Double Punch (right then left)
Cane Held: Natural Grip

1. Step right foot forward to the right: execute an outside block to the inside of the attacker's right forearm.

2. Rotate the wrist toward the right and drive the shaft straight across to block the inside of the attacker's left arm.

3. Grasp the shaft at the end-grip with the left hand (palm away), and slide the cane forward and up so that the tip end extends beyond the attacker's neck from their left side, and rotate your right wrist so the crook turns upward to hook around the attacker's left wrist or forearm.

4. Pull down on the shaft of the cane with the left hand toward the left hip while raising the right hand (so the crook end is high)

CT-50

Attack: Right Punch

Cane Held: Reverse Mid-Shaft Grip

1. Step forward into a LFS: execute a left knife hand block.

2. Execute a vertical punch with the right hand holding the cane.

3. Rotate the right hand (palm-up) so the shaft is at an angle across the front of the attacker's body with the crook end high to the attacker's left side.

4. Step right foot up and left foot around behind the attacker's right leg, turning into the attacker. Reach the left arm under the attacker's right arm and around their upper back to grab the shaft of the cane near the crook (palm-down).

5. Release the right hand. The tip end of the shaft now lies behind your left hip and across the front of the attacker.

6. Pull back on the cane with your left hand to apply pressure. The right hand is prepared to execute a strike.

Safety: Be aware that the shaft can create great pressure on the collar bone or chest.

CT-51

Attack: End of Shaft grabbed with 2 hands
Cane Held: Natural Grip

1. Grab shaft with the left hand from underneath (palm-up) near the attacker's hands. You many step forward, as needed.

2. Circle the shaft clockwise, first toward the left then up and over top of the attacker's wrists and then straight down on the attacker's wrists toward your right side.

CT-52

Attack: End of Shaft grabbed with 2 hands

Cane Held: Natural Grip

1. Step left foot forward. Grab shaft with the left hand from the top (palm-down) near the attacker's hands.

2. Pull the shaft slightly toward your right (so that the attacker reacts to pull it back away from you).

3. As the attacker pulls back to try to gain control of the cane, release your left grip and counter with a back fist to the attacker's head.

CT-53

Attack: Sleeve Grab (arm holding cane)
Cane Held: Natural Grip

1. Raise your right arm up so your right forearm touches the inside of the attacker's left forearm, with the crook extending to the right side beyond the attacker's forearm.

2. Pull your right hand down to apply leverage with the shaft near the crook on the attacker's forearm to create a bend in their arm, completing trapping technique.

3. Step your left foot across to the right between you and the attacker, and grab the end-grip palm-down.

4. Bring your left hand up to strike the right side of the attacker's neck with the shaft to compete a takedown.

CT-54

Attack: #3 strike with a cane

Cane Held: Natural Grip

1. Step forward to the right: execute a reinforced outside block to intercept the attacker's cane at mid-shaft with your left palm pressing near the intersection of the canes.

2. Raise your right hand to position the shaft over the attacker's right thumb (crook end), and grasp both shafts near the crook. Simultaneously, grasp both shafts (palm down) mid-shaft. Safety: use light pressure with a partner as this move can create a great deal of force on the thumb.

3. Bring the right hand in a CW motion down toward the right and under the attackers forearm, then up and onto the attacker's right wrist.

4. The canes will be parallel with the floor and horizontal in front of you at hip height, turning the attacker's wrist over.

CT-55

Attack: #3 strike with a cane/stick

Cane Held: Natural Grip

1. Step forward to the right: execute a reinforced outside block to intercept the attacker's cane at mid-shaft with your left palm pressing near the intersection of the canes.

2. Raise your right hand to position the shaft over the attacker's right thumb (crook end), and grasp both shafts near the crook. Simultaneously, grasp both shafts (palm down) mid-shaft. <u>Safety</u>: use light pressure with a partner as this move can create a great deal of force on the thumb.

3. Bring the right hand down and under the attacker's right arm in a circular motion.

4. Continue the motion by directing the crook upward from behind the attacker's arm to their right side as you step the right foot past the attacker's left side.

5. Continuing the flow, step the left foot around turning into the attacker from behind, and continue the right hand's circular motion to hook the attacker's right forearm with one of the crooks from below. Simultaneously, bring the left hand up (palm away) so the cane shafts' are vertical with tips up.

6. Release the left hand and reach around the attacker's neck from their left side and grab the upper shafts of the canes (palm away) on the right side of the attacker's neck.

<u>Safety</u>: be careful around your partner's neck and thumb.

CT-56

Attack: Low Knife Lunge

Cane Held: Natural Grip

1. Step forward into a LFS: execute a low shaft block (both hands grabbing cane, palm-down) onto the attacker's right hand.

2. Execute a horizontal shaft strike to the attacker's face or throat.

3. Release the left hand, and execute a low strike to the side of the attacker's knee.

CT-57

Attack: Right Punch

Cane Held: Chambered Reverse Crook Grip

1. Execute a left knife hand block to the inside of the attacker's right wrist, then slide down to grab the attacker's right wrist (palm down).

2. Hook the attacker's right elbow joint with the horn and crook of the cane from underneath by bringing the cane up to your left under the attacker's arm. The shaft should remain chambered to your right side, and your right forearm may make contact with the attacker's arm.

3. Pull the right hand and crook down toward your right side, bending the attacker's elbow and pulling the joint to the right. Simultaneously, lift the attacker's right wrist up and then push it back and down past the attacker's right shoulder for takedown.

CT-58

Attack: #12 strike with a cane/stick

Cane Held: Natural Grip

1. Step into a RFS: execute a high block, blocking the attacker's cane mid-shaft. The left hand remains as a guard.

2. Raise the left hand up (palm away) to the outside of your cane to the right of the attacker's cane, and execute a clearing technique by sliding your left forearm down the shaft of your cane to the left, catching the attacker's cane and grabbing the shaft in your left hand. Simultaneously, begin to draw the shaft of your cane toward the right.

3. Complete the motion by executing a high strike to the left side of the attacker's head (bring the shaft overhead and around from the right), while bringing your left hand and the attacker's cane to your left hip.

CT-59

Attack: #12 strike with a cane/stick

Cane Held: Natural Grip

1. Step into a RFS: execute a reverse high block, blocking the attacker's cane mid-shaft. The left hand remains as a guard.

2. Redirect the shaft of the attacker's cane to the right by checking it with your left hand (outside your left arm). Rotate right wrist palm down into a high strike (palm down) to the right side of the attacker's head, bringing the shaft around from overhead and then from your left.

CT-60

Attack: Low Knife Lunge

Cane Held: Natural Grip

1. Step right foot to the right: execute an outside block on top of the attacker's right wrist.

2. Grasp the shaft at the end-grip with your left hand (palm down), step right foot forward, and execute a strike with the crook to the left side of the attacker's jaw.

CT-61

Attack: Low Knife Lunge

Cane Held: Natural Grip

1. Step left foot to the left: execute a right center block.

2. Pivot on the left foot, stepping CW with the right foot, grasping the cane with both hands palm-down, and execute a crook strike the attacker's spine.

3. Step the left foot around CW to face the attacker from behind. Execute a high strike (palm down).

CT-62

Attack: Low Knife Lunge

Cane Held: Natural Grip

1. Step right foot to the right: execute an outside block on top of the attacker's right wrist.

2. Step right foot forward. Pull cane shaft out to the right. Execute a high strike to the left side of the attacker's head.

CT-63

Attack: Low Knife Lunge

Cane Held: Natural Grip

1. Step forward into a LFS: execute tip strike to the attacker's right ribcage.

2. Bring the cane around in a circular motion (start motion by lowering the cane): execute an overhead strike to the head.

CT-64

Attack: Overhead Knife Attack

Cane Held: Two-Handed Grip

1. Step right foot forward into RFS and execute a high shaft block to the attacker's forearm.

2. Step left foot to the right and execute a low strike to the attacker's knee.

CT-65

Attack: Double Lapel Grab

Cane Held: Reverse Crook Grip

1. Slide your right hand down the shaft until it is just below the crook on the grip with the horn forward.

2. Bring the crook up between the attacker's arms (toward the left), and place the horn on the attacker's right scapula, and grip the upper crook with your left hand.

3. Pull straight down.

CT-66

Attack: Double Lapel Grab

Cane Held: Crook Grip

1. Grasp the shaft in your left hand (palm down), and execute a tip strike onto the attacker's right instep by driving the right hand down and allowing the shaft to slide through the left hand.

2. Position the shaft over the attacker's arms clockwise by bringing the left hand over the top of the attacker's arms from the left toward the right, allowing the left hand grip to loosen slightly (the left hand is rotated palm up). The right hand is rotated palm up and across the front of your body to your left.

3. Pull your left hand down toward your left hip (so the shaft catches the left side of the attacker's neck). The right hand and shaft will rotate CCW as part of this motion.

CT-67

Attack: Right Punch

Cane Held: Mid-Shaft Grip

1. Step into a LFS: execute a left knife hand block and an outside block (crook up) to the inside of the attacker's right arm.

2. Rotate your right wrist so the crook points toward your right and hook the crook around the right side of the attacker's neck (toward the right).

3. Grab the attacker's right wrist with your left hand.

4. Step the right foot between you and the attacker, turning your body CCW, as you step under the attacker's right arm.

5. Step the left foot backwards under the attacker's right arm and bring the shaft over your head to the front of your body as you move past the attacker's right side.

6. Pull upward on the attacker's wrist and press the shaft downward on the back of the attacker's arm.

CT-68

Attack: Right Punch

Cane Held: Mid-Shaft Grip

1. Step into a RFS: execute a left knife hand block and an outside block (crook up) to the inside of the attacker's right arm.

2. Rotate your right wrist so the crook points toward your right and hook the crook around the right side of the attacker's neck (toward the right).

3. Grab the attacker's right wrist with your left hand.

4. Bring the attacker's right arm across the front of your body to the right (under the cane).

5. Step your left foot across between you and the attacker and lower your hips so that you can step under your cane, raising the shaft over your head and turn to face the attacker.

6. Bring the attacker's right hand over the shaft, and pull the shaft.

CT-69

Attack: Rear Choke Hold (from Right)

Cane Held: Seated: Reverse Crook Grip

1. Bring the cane up to your right (allowing your left hand to slide down the shaft toward the tip end) and hook the attacker around the right side of their neck (similar to CT-18).

2. Pull on the shaft down toward your front right side (sliding the right hand up toward the crook end and the attacker's neck for better control) for a takedown.

CT-70

Attack: Headlock (from Right)
Cane Held: Reverse Crook Grip

1. Slide hand down shaft into a mid-shaft grip.

2. Raise your right hand up from behind the attacker's left arm (which is around your neck) and bring the shaft between you and the attacker's head (with the crook facing toward your right).

3. Pull up to hook the crook under the attacker's throat and pull down on the shaft to apply leverage under the attacker's chin.

4. As the attacker arcs back and begins to rise, stand with the attacker, continuing the pressure downward on the shaft.

CT-71

Attack: Headlock (from Right)

Cane Held: Reverse Crook Grip

1. Slide right hand down to a mid-shaft grip, and bend at the knees (stepping wider as needed).

2. Bring the shaft of the cane between the attacker's legs with the crook to the front and grab it with the left hand (palm down) near the attacker's left shin. The shaft is positioned so it lies along the shin on the inside of the leg and your hands are close.

3. Pull on the shaft (slightly upwards) to apply pressure for a compliance response.

CT-72

Attack: Headlock (from Left) to Knees

Cane Held: Reverse Crook Grip

1. As the headlock is applied, kneel down. The left knee is down (closest to the attacker) and the right knee up; however, it is acceptable to reverse this position. Simultaneously, slide the hand down to a mid-shaft grip.

2. Strike the attacker's shin (normally their left leg, which is farthest from you, but it may be either) with the shaft to your left. The crook should point to the back.

3. Pull on the shaft to the right to hook the attacker's leg with the crook. Simultaneously, push into the attacker's right ribs with your left palm in the opposite direction for a takedown.

CT-73

Attack: Right Punch (or reach to grab)
Cane Held: Seated: Mid-Shaft Grip

1. Execute a left knife hand block to the inside of the attacker's right wrist. Simultaneously, strike upward with the crook under the attacker's jaw.

2. Bring your right hand back near your right shoulder to level the cane parallel to the floor with the tip pointed toward the attacker and grab the shaft near the end-grip with your left hand.

3. Execute a tip strike into the attacker's chest by driving both hands and the cane forward.

CT-74

Attack: Right Punch

Cane Held: Seated: Natural Grip across Thighs

1. Lean your body slightly to the right to avoid the attacker's right punch: execute a high shaft block into the attacker's right arm (both hands palms down).

2. Bring shaft back to chest area and then lean forward slightly to drive the mid-shaft of the cane downward into the attacker's right knee.

CT-75

Attack: Right Punch

Cane Held: Seated: Natural Grip across Thighs

1. Lean your body slightly to the right to avoid the attacker's right punch: execute a low shaft strike down into the attacker's right knee.

2. Bring the shaft back to the chest, and execute a shaft strike to the attacker's face, angling the cane slightly (crook slightly higher to your right).

Advanced CTs

The first 75 CTs are required to test for first degree black belt. There are additional CTs at the black belt levels. Some of these are for the Walking Staff, Umbrella, White Cane, and others. However, more common are general self-defense techniques and concepts. Some of these are for working with individuals with mobility challenges or who are blind or visually impaired. These techniques are not available in this textbook.

CHAPTER 10
FORMS

INTRODUCTION TO FORMS
BASIC CANE KATA
REFLECTION 1-5
NATURAL WALK
BLACK BELT FORMS

Forms

Forms, by definition in the "Overlook Martial Arts Dictionary," are a predetermined pattern of movements synonymous with almost every martial art. Known in Japanese as *kata* (formal exercise), in Korean as *hyung* (pattern), and in Chinese as *kuen*. In the United States the basic term "forms" is used, or most commonly "kata."

Another aspect of forms is the fact that they are a series of movements that must be done the same way by each individual each time the form is done.

Forms are based on a series of motions that are executed in the effort to fight off imaginary opponents. Most of the moves are punches, kicks, and blocks, but some moves are transitional moves. Transitional moves are done for various reasons. For example, you have just executed a center block reverse punch and neutralized that particular attacker, but as you turn to look for the next attacker, you execute a knife hand block. The concept is that you should fall into a defensive posture while looking and turning.

Forms serve other purposes. Hundreds of years ago they allowed students to practice their style and what their instructor had taught them over long periods of time away from formal instruction. Even now forms allow students of a school and style to keep the style alive even if they must move hundreds of miles from their instructor or if the instructor should pass away.

Forms challenge the balance of a student's mind with their body and the balance between power and flow. Many martial artists consider forms the backbone and, in turn, the future survival of a style.

In the early forms the moves are done at one second per move. As you go up in levels of difficulty some of the katas for brown belt level will have a change in timing of a technique. Once in the black belt forms the one-second per move is replaced with the added difficulty of understanding timing and its relationship to flow. In all forms the challenge is to acquire a balance between flow and power. Neither is to become the controlling factor for the form. For a person to be successful in something that they are doing, their subconscious and conscious mind must be in balance and both committed to the task. Sometimes the term balance leads the student to feel that a fifty/fifty breakdown in the amount of involvement is what is being called for. This is not the case in some high rank colored belt forms and definitely not the case in black belt forms. Each kata is to be done the same by each black belt in moves and direction, but not necessarily in the speed of movement (flow) and execution of power. It should be obvious that each person is different in body size, flexibility, strength, as well as age, sex and personality. All of these factors change the execution of what percentage of flow is mixed with what percentage of power. It is this mixture that places the life in a form and results in a powerful as well as a beautiful kata. Not all of the forms done in the American Eagle Cane Style are available in this instructional textbook.

Introduction to the Reflection Forms

There are five Reflection Forms and all five of them are done in this style of martial arts. These forms integrate traditional movements of this style of martial arts, but also create a skill level that is increased and enhanced as you move through each one during your training. Formulated by Masters Stalloch and Crandall, the Reflection forms are now done by other schools. They appear on the American Cane System eight DVD series, performed and taught by Masters Stalloch, Crandall, and Jessee. Reflection 1 may also be performed from a wheelchair, as documented on the DVD Cane-Fu: Moving Beyond Disabilities. It should also be kept in mind that there are other series of forms that can be done to gradually develop a person's martial arts skills. That means that there are empty-hand styles that do the Pal-Gwes, while others do the Heians or even the Taegeuks. There are a series of growth forms in Japanese and Chinese styles as well as many other martial arts styles in the world.

For those that do the Reflection Forms you may see some slight differences depending on the original master teaching or the book they emanated from. Slight changes are normal, but the form direction and stances should be the same no matter which school does these forms. One of the biggest differences seen from one school to the next is not in the technique, but what it is called. For some an outside block is called an inside block and the reverse also holds true. This is because some stylists identify the techniques by standing with their arms to their sides with palms facing front. That means whenever they strike with the part of their arm that is closest to the side of their body they call it an inside block. And if the part of their arm to the outside of their body is used, they call that an outside block. Other stylists stand with their arms to their sides, but with palms facing back. This reverses which part of their arm is now on the inside for an inside block and the part of their arm which is outside for outside blocks. American Eagle Cane stylists stand with their arms to the sides with palms back, which determines the names used for inside and outside blocks as they are extended into the cane.

Your instructor should first show you your new form and assist you with some of the more unique aspects of the new form.

You should not be skipping forms to higher ones or you will miss out on the building process that they were designed for.

218

THE REFLECTION KATAS

Reflection contains a dual meaning. First, it refers to the structure of the kata. Each reflection kata is performed starting with the cane in the right hand. Once the form reaches its midpoint the same moves are repeated as mirror image with the cane starting in the left hand. This brings a symmetry to the form and to the physical skills of the body. Second, it refers to an image of tranquil water casting a reflection. Through traditional kata we seek to develop discipline and bring unity to the mind and body. As the mind becomes calm and clear, it reflects our inner self. Reflection 1, 2, and 5 are an I pattern. Reflection 3 is an I pattern with a cross bar near the top of the form. Reflection 4 is a T pattern.

BLACK BELT FORMS

This section deals with some of the black belt forms. These forms have not been elaborated on and are presented as a guide to assist black belts who have already been shown the form by their instructor.

There are many idiosyncrasies and quirks to these forms that, to be done correctly, require the assistance of your instructor. These forms are covered in detail at the instructors' classes, which gives each instructor an opportunity to ask questions and take notes to understand the form and clarify the most productive method of teaching the form. Non-instructor black belts receive their training in these forms in regular classes, as do all other ranks regarding their forms.

As an American Style we have the luxury to span the vast wealth of knowledge that exists in the traditions of the Japanese, Korean and Chinese styles. Through our travels we have been fortunate to have shared time and knowledge with very wise and experienced Masters and have made it our aim to keep alive the history and traditions of their forms and techniques. The following forms are presented in the order required for belt rank and give the participating student a growing skill level in many facets of the martial arts. All of the forms listed exist in written form in this textbook.

Regarding black belt testings, only the forms required for each rank are listed below; the rest of the required material can be learned by talking to your instructor. Although there are many additional requirements for each rank, the following identifies the *forms* which are required.

Required Black Belt Forms

First Degree:

Basic Cane Kata, Reflections 1-5, Natural Walk, and Anvil

Second Degree:

Autumn Wind

Third Degree:

Briar Patch (with Walking Staff / BoCane)

Fourth Degree:

Valley

Fifth Degree:

Old Man with a Cane

Sixth Degree:

Must design and document a traditional cane kata which will become part of the style's future growth. This kata must be approved by the Headmaster.

Seventh Degree:

Minimum of one Kata designed by Master Instructors may be learned.

Eighth Degree:

All Katas designed by Master instructors must be learned.

Basic Cane Kata

In the following pictures, Front and Back refer to the perspective of an observer standing at D, facing A.

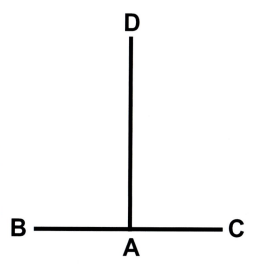

Ready Stance:

Starting at A, facing D, Ready Stance (Chumbi) with cane chambered under right arm in crook grip. Allow crook to rotate in your hand so the tip rests on the floor at your right side. Slide your right hand down to a natural grip, and raise the tip off the floor.

READY STANCE   NATURAL GRIP   LOOK BEFORE YOU TURN

Toward B

1. Pivot 90° counterclockwise toward B into LFS: Execute a reinforced high block.

2. Step right foot forward into RFS: Execute a low strike.

1: FRONT VIEW   2: FRONT VIEW

Toward C

3. Turn 180° clockwise toward C into RFS: Execute a reinforced high block.

4. Step left foot forward into LFS: Execute a lunge strike.

LOOK BEFORE YOU TURN   3: FRONT VIEW   4: FRONT VIEW

Toward D

5. Turn 90° counterclockwise toward D and step into LFS: Execute a reinforced down block.

LOOK BEFORE YOU TURN   5: FRONT VIEW

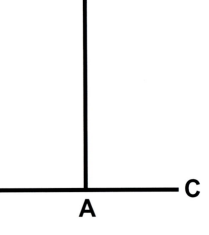

6. Step right foot forward into RFS: Execute a high block.

7. Step left foot forward into LFS: Execute a center block.

8. Step right foot forward into RFS: Execute a high strike (#5). **[YELL]**

6: FRONT VIEW

7: FRONT VIEW

8: FRONT VIEW

Maintain stance, switch cane to left hand natural grip. **NOTE**: the remaining techniques of the kata are performed with the cane in the _left_ hand.

Toward A

9. Turn 180° clockwise toward A and step into RFS: Execute a reinforced down block.

LOOK BEFORE YOU TURN

9: FRONT VIEW

9:BACK VIEW

223

10. Step left foot forward into LFS: Execute a high block.

11. Step right foot forward into RFS: Execute a center block.

12. Step left foot forward into a LFS: Execute a high strike (#5 strike). **[YELL]**

10: FRONT VIEW

11: FRONT VIEW

12: FRONT VIEW

10: BACK VIEW

11: BACK VIEW

12: BACK VIEW

13A. Take a step forward with your right foot: this is a transitional posture to prepare for the next turn.

13A:
BACK VIEW

13A: FRONT VIEW

LOOK BEFORE YOU TURN

Toward B

13B. Turn 270° counterclockwise toward B and step into LFS: Execute a reinforced high block.

14. Step forward into RFS: Execute low strike.

13B: FRONT VIEW

14: FRONT VIEW

<u>Toward C</u>

15. Turn 180°clockwise into RFS: Execute a reinforced high block.

16. Step forward into LFS: Execute a lunge strike. **[YELL]**

LOOK BEFORE YOU TURN   15: FRONT VIEW   16: FRONT VIEW

Ready Stance (Chumbi): Bring left foot back toward your right foot to stand facing D, switch the cane back to the right hand in a crook grip chambered under your right arm.

SWITCH HANDS   STANDING   READY STANCE

REFLECTION 1

Standing at A

Ready Stance (Chumbi) / Switch to natural grip

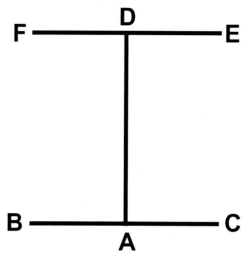

Toward B:

1. Step left foot into LFS toward B: Reinforced down block / Low strike (#1).

2. RFS toward B: Mid-shaft strike (both palms down).

Toward C:

3. Turn CCW 180° into LFS toward C: Reinforced down block / Low strike (#1).

4. RFS toward C: Mid-shaft strike (both palms down).

Toward D:

5. Pivot on balls of feet CCW 90° into a LFS toward D: Parry block (right to left) / Redirection technique (turn right palm up, cane ends horizontal).

6. RFS toward D: High strike (#5). **[YELL]**

7. LFS toward D: High block.

8. RFS toward D: #2 low strike / #12 overhead strike (from left shoulder). **[YELL]**

Toward E:

9. Turn CCW 270° into LFS toward E: Left knife hand block and low strike (#1) (block and strike executed simultaneously).

10. RFS toward E: Mid-shaft strike (both palms down).

Toward F:

11. Turn CCW 180° into LFS toward F: Left knife hand block and low strike (#1) (block and strike executed simultaneously).

12. RFS toward F: Mid-shaft strike (both palms down).

Toward A:

13. Pivot on balls of feet CCW 90°into LFS toward A: Left knife hand block / Interweave technique (right hand ends near right shoulder with cane tip extending backwards, upper body angled slightly toward the left).

14. RBS toward A: Leverage technique – performed similar to high strike (#5), bring left hand to chamber.

15. LFS toward A: Center block.

16. RFS toward A: Low strike to your right side.

Toward D:

17. Pivot on right foot bringing left foot around CW 180° toward D: #12 overhead strike (from left side). **[YELL]**

18. Step left foot <u>up to right</u> into a standing posture, switching cane to left hand in a natural grip.

Repeat the mirror image of techniques 1 - 18 as follows:

Toward C:

19. Step right foot into RFS toward C: Reinforced down block / Low strike (#1).

20. LFS toward C: Mid-shaft strike (both palms down).

Toward B:

21. Turn CW 180° into RFS toward B: Reinforced down block / Low strike (#1).

22. LFS toward B: Mid-shaft strike (both palms down).

Toward D:

23. Pivot on balls of feet CW 90° into a RFS toward D: Parry block (left to right) / Redirection technique (turn left palm up, cane ends horizontal).

24. LFS toward D: High strike (#5). **[YELL]**

25. RFS toward D: High block.

26. LFS toward D: #2 low strike / #12 overhead strike (from right shoulder). **[YELL]**

228

Toward F:

27. Turn CW 270° into RFS toward F: Right knife hand block and low strike (#1) (block and strike executed simultaneously).

28. LFS toward F: Mid-shaft strike (both palms down).

Toward E:

29. Turn CW 180° into RFS toward E: Right knife hand block and low strike (#1) (block and strike executed simultaneously).

30. LFS toward E: Mid-shaft strike (both palms down).

Toward A:

31. Pivot on balls of feet CW 90° into RFS toward A: Right knife hand block / Interweave technique (left hand ends near left shoulder with cane tip extending backwards, upper body angled slightly toward the right).

32. LBS toward A: Leverage technique – performed as a high strike (#5), bring right hand to chamber.

33. RFS toward A: Center block.

34. LFS toward A: Low strike to your left side.

Toward D:

35. Pivot on left foot bringing right foot around CCW 180° toward D: #12 overhead strike (from right side). **[YELL]**

36. Step right foot up to left into a standing posture, switching cane to the right hand in a crook grip that is chambered under the right arm.

Ready Stance (Chumbi)

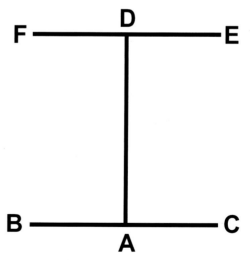

REFLECTION 2

Standing at A

Ready Stance (Chumbi) / Switch to crook grip with tip on floor

```
F ———————————————— E
          D
          |
          |
          |
          |
          |
          |
B ———————————————— C
          A
```

Toward D

1. Step left foot back into RBS facing D: Low parry block (right to left) / high swing strike (left to right).

Toward B

2. Move left foot to turn 90° CCW into LFS toward B: Figure-8 (right to left, left to right), chamber cane (horn down).

3. RFS toward B: Left knife hand block / Right cane punch (horn down), left hand returns to chamber / Horn strike (extend cane high diagonally to left, grasp shaft with left hand, pull down toward right chamber). Note: Bring cane shaft to outside of right arm on transition into next stance.

Toward C

4. Turn CCW 180° into LFS toward C: Figure-8 (right to left, left to right), chamber cane (horn down).

5. RFS toward C: Left knife hand block / Right cane punch (horn down), left hand returns to chamber / Horn strike (see move 3).

Toward D

6. Move right foot to turn 90° CCW into RBS toward D: Slide right hand down to Natural Grip and execute a parry block (right to left).

7. Step left foot CCW 180° into HS toward D (left foot leads, body faces E/C side): Execute a strike with the tip of cane to the back on left side (double shaft grip, both palms down).

8. RFS toward D: Reinforced high block / Left low center kick (set kick back down into RFS) / #12 overhead strike (strike comes from right shoulder). **[YELL]**

230

Toward F

9. Pivot 90° CCW on balls of feet into LFS toward F: Reverse high block / Mid strike (#4). Note: the shaft of the cane angles slightly to the left.

10. RFS toward F: Lunge strike to solar plexus (left palm up).

Toward E

11. Move left foot to turn 180° CCW into LFS toward E: Reverse high block / Mid strike (#4). Note: the shaft of the cane angles slightly to the left.

12. RFS toward E: Lunge strike to solar plexus (left palm up).

Toward A

13. Turn 90° CW by sliding right foot over into RBS toward A: Vertical block (left to right). Note: This is done by switching the left hand grip to palm down and raising the left hand up (both hands grip palm-down).

14. Step left foot into HS toward A: Shaft-end takedown (double-handed grip, palms down: reach tip out to left side, pull down to left chamber).

15. RFS toward A: Reinforced high block / Left low center kick (set kick back down into RFS) / #12 overhead strike (strike comes from right shoulder). **[YELL]**

Toward D

16. Move left foot to turn CCW 180° into LFS toward D: Left knife hand block / Low strike (#1). **[YELL]**

17. Bring left foot *back to right* into a standing posture, switching cane to left hand into a crook grip.

Repeat the mirror image of techniques 1 - 17 as follows:

Toward D

18. Step right foot back into LBS facing D: Low parry block (left to right) / High swing strike (right to left).

Toward C

19. Move right foot to turn 90° CW into RFS toward C: Figure-8 (left to right, right to left), chamber cane (horn down).

20. LFS toward C: Right knife hand block / Left cane punch (horn down), right hand returns to chamber / Horn strike (extend cane high diagonally to right, grasp shaft with right hand, pull down toward the left chamber). Note: Bring cane shaft to outside of left arm on transition into next stance.

Toward B

21. Turn CW 180° into RFS toward B: Figure-8 (left to right, right to left), chamber cane (horn down).

22. LFS toward B: Right knife hand block / Left cane punch (horn down), right hand returns to chamber / Horn strike (see move 20).

Toward D

23. Move left foot to turn 90° CW into LBS toward D: Slide left hand down to Natural Grip and execute a parry block (left to right).

24. Step right foot CW 180° into HS toward D (right foot leads, body faces F/B side): Execute a strike with the tip of cane to the back on right side (double shaft grip, both palms down).

25. LFS toward D: Reinforced high block / Right low center kick (set kick back down into LFS) / #12 overhead strike (strike comes from left shoulder). **[YELL]**

Toward E

26. Pivot 90° CW on balls of feet into RFS toward E: Reverse high block / Mid strike (#4). Note: The shaft of the cane angles slightly to the right.

27. LFS toward E: Lunge strike to solar plexus (right palm up).

Toward F

28. Move right foot to turn 180° CW into RFS toward F: Reverse high block / Mid strike (#4). Note: The shaft of the cane angles slightly to the right.

29. LFS toward F: Lunge strike to solar plexus (right palm up).

Toward A

30. Turn 90° CCW by sliding left foot over into LBS toward A: Vertical block (right to left). Note: This is done by switching the right hand grip to palm down and raising the right hand up (both hands grip palm-down).

31. Step right foot into HS toward A: Shaft-end takedown (double-handed grip, palms down, reach tip out to right side, pull down to right chamber).

32. LFS toward A: Reinforced high block / Right low center kick (set kick back down into LFS) / #12 overhead strike (strike comes from left shoulder). **[YELL]**

Toward D

33. Move right foot to turn CW 180° into RFS toward D: Right knife hand block / Low strike (#1). **[YELL]**

34. Bring right foot *back to left* into a standing posture, switching cane to right hand into a chambered position.

Ready Stance (Chumbi)

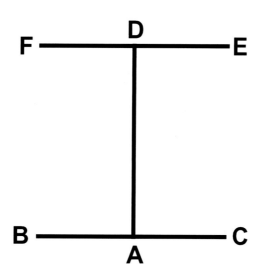

REFLECTION 3

Reflection 3 involves many sweeping techniques and challenges flow. Consult your instructor for the subtleties, timing, and flow for this kata.

Standing at A

Ready Stance (Chumbi) / Switch to natural grip

Toward D

1. Maintain standing posture facing D: Execute high shaft block (both hands closed on shaft) / Right low strike (#1). Left hand released into a guard.

2. Drop left foot back into RFS and execute #2 strike (circling overhead left to right).

Toward B

3. Pivot 90° CCW into LFS toward B: Tip strike to solar plexus.

4A. Step forward into RFS: #7 strike from right to left (following through to left hip).

4B. Maintain RFS: Right high block / Left hand clearing technique with right #5 strike which follows through to left hip.

Toward C

5. Turn 180° CCW into LFS toward C: Tip strike to solar plexus.

6A. Step forward into RFS: #7 strike following through to left hip.

6B. Maintain RFS: Right high block / Left hand clearing technique with right #5 strike which follows through to left hip.

Toward D

7. Pivot 90° CCW into LFS toward D: Reinforced parry block (left to right). Note: left hand reinforces (fingers to front).

8. Step forward into RFS: Double-handed crook strike to the neck (right to left). Left hand grasps the lower shaft, right hand releases and grasps above the left hand / Pull down with the left hand and slide the right hand up the shaft near the crook and simultaneously execute a left knee strike to the solar plexus.

9A. Step down into LFS: Takedown technique. Completed by bringing the tip of the cane (left hand) down from left to right and bringing the right hand and crook near the right hip (driving the attacker down and releasing their neck from the crook).

9B. Maintain LFS: #12 strike with back of crook (horn facing you). Completed by sliding right hand down shaft to left hand. **[YELL]**

Toward E

10. Pivot 90° CW into RFS toward E: Pull the cane with the left hand so the right hand slides into a reverse crook grip with the cane on the left side of the body / execute horizontal middle swing strike (left to right).

11. Bring left foot up onto ball of the foot near right foot: Execute 2 overhead twirls / Step into deep LFS: Horizontal high swing strike (right to left).

Toward F

12. Turn 180° CW into RFS toward F: Horizontal middle swing strike (left to right).

13. Bring left foot up onto ball of the foot near right foot: Execute 2 overhead twirls / Step into deep LFS: Horizontal high swing strike (right to left).

Toward G

14. Pivot 90° CW into RFS toward G: Horizontal middle swing strike (left to right) / ½ of a figure-8 (right high to left low) / reverse the horn (left to right) to a crook grip that ends to the front right of the body.

15. Low left roundhouse instep kick toward G (body facing H). Tip is on the floor during the kick.

Toward H

16. Set the left leg down into RFS toward H: Brace block.

17. Step into LFS: Level the cane and execute short lunge strike (right hand on the crook, left hand palm-down mid-shaft).

18. Step into RFS: Release right hand, grab above the left hand, and execute a #12 strike with the back of the crook (horn faces you). This grip is close to mid-shaft and a shorter strike than in move 9B.

19. Step back into LFS: Level the cane, release the right hand, and re-grab the end of the crook as in move 17.

Toward I

20. Turn 180° CW into RFS facing I: Brace block.

21. Step into LFS: Level the cane and execute short lunge strike (right hand on the crook, left hand palm-down mid-shaft).

22. Step into RFS: Release right hand, grab above the left hand, and execute a #12 strike with the back of the crook (horn faces you). Note: this grip is close to mid-shaft and a shorter strike than in move 12.

23. Step back into LFS: Level the cane, release the right hand, and re-grab cane **near the crook palm-down.**

Moving Toward A / Facing G

24. Pivot 90° CW into RFS toward G: Execute a reinforced high block.

25. Step back into LFS: Reinforced down block.

26. Step back into RFS: Reinforced center block.

27. Step back into LFS: Reinforced parry block (right to left). Note: reinforced by left open palm-away, fingers up.

28. Step back into RFS: #12 overhead strike from left shoulder. **[YELL]**

Step right foot back to left into standing posture, switching cane to left hand natural grip.

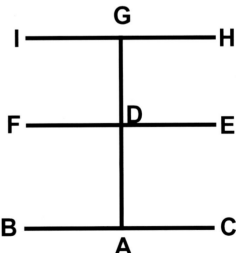

Repeat the mirror image of techniques 1 - 28 as follows:

Toward D

29. Maintain standing posture facing D: Execute high shaft block (both hands closed on shaft) / Left low strike (#1). Note: right hand released into a guard.

30. Drop right foot back into LFS and execute #2 strike (circling overhead right to left).

Toward C

31. Pivot 90° CW into RFS toward C: Tip strike to solar plexus.

32A. Step forward into LFS: #7 strike from left to right following through to right hip.

32B. Maintain LFS: Left high block / Right hand clearing technique with left #5 strike which follows through to right hip.

Toward B

33. Turn 180° CW into RFS toward B: Tip strike to solar plexus.

34A. Step forward into LFS: #7 strike following through to right hip.

34B. Maintain LFS: Left high block / Right hand clearing technique with left #5 strike which follows through to right hip.

Toward D

35. Pivot 90° CW into RFS toward D: Reinforced parry block (right to left). Right hand reinforces (fingers to front).

36. Step forward into LFS: Double-handed crook strike to the neck (left to right). Right hand grasps the lower shaft, left hand releases and grasps above the right hand / Pull down with the right hand and slide the left hand up the shaft near the crook and simultaneously execute a right knee strike to the solar plexus.

37A. Step down into RFS: Takedown technique. Note: completed by bringing the tip of the cane (right hand) down from right to left and bringing the left hand and crook near the left hip (driving the attacker down and releasing their neck from the crook).

37B. Maintain RFS: #12 strike with back of the crook (horn facing you). Completed by sliding left hand down shaft to right hand. **[YELL]**

Toward F

38. Pivot 90° CCW into LFS toward F: Pull the cane with the right hand so the left hand slides into a reverse crook grip with the cane on the right side of the body / Execute horizontal middle swing strike (right to left).

39. Bring right foot up onto ball of the foot near left foot: Execute 2 overhead twirls / Step into deep RFS: Horizontal high swing strike (left to right).

Toward E

40. Turn 180° CCW into LFS toward E: Horizontal middle swing strike (right to left).

41. Bring right foot up onto ball of the foot near left foot: Execute 2 overhead twirls / Step into deep RFS: Horizontal high swing strike (left to right).

Toward G

42. Pivot 90° CCW into LFS toward G: Horizontal middle swing strike (right to left) / ½ of a figure-8 (left high to right low) / reverse the horn (right to left) to a crook grip that ends to the front left of the body.

43. Low right roundhouse instep kick toward G (body facing I). Tip of cane is on the floor during the kick.

Toward I

44. Set the right leg down into LFS toward I: Brace block.

45. Step into RFS: Level the cane and execute short lunge strike (left hand on the crook, right hand palm-down mid-shaft).

46. Step into LFS: Release left hand, grab above the right hand, and execute a #12 strike with the back of the crook (horn faces you). This grip is close to mid-shaft and a shorter strike than in move 37B.

47. Step back into RFS: Level the cane, release the left hand, and re-grab the end of the crook as in move 45.

Toward H

48. Turn 180° CCW into LFS facing H: Brace block.

49. Step into RFS: Level the cane and execute short lunge strike (left hand on the crook, right hand palm-down mid-shaft).

50. Step into LFS: Release left hand, grab above the right hand, and execute a #12 strike with the back of the crook (horn faces you). Note: this grip is close to mid-shaft and a shorter strike than in move 44.

51. Step back into RFS: Level the cane, release the left hand, and re-grab cane **near the crook palm-down**.

Moving Toward A / Facing G

52. Pivot 90° CCW into LFS toward G: Execute a reinforced high block.

53. Step back into RFS: Reinforced down block.

54. Step back into LFS: Reinforced center block.

55. Step back into RFS: Reinforced parry block (left to right). Note: reinforced by right open palm-away, fingers up.

56. Step back into LFS: #12 overhead strike from right shoulder. **[YELL]**

Step left foot back to right into standing posture, switching cane from left hand to right crook grip, chambered).

Ready Stance (Chumbi)

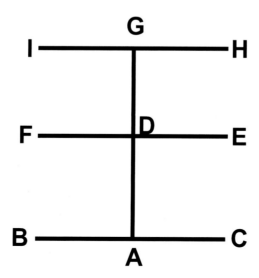

REFLECTION 4

Standing at A

Ready Stance (Chumbi) / Switch to natural grip.

Toward B

1A. Step forward into LFS: Execute reinforced center block (left to right).

1B. Switch to a double-shaft grip: Execute upward crook strike to lower ribs / downward shaft strike (near tip) to head.

2. Pivot on balls of feet 45° CW into HS: Execute horizontal shaft strike (chest high)

3A. Step forward into RFS: Execute reinforced outside block (right to left).

3B. Switch to a double-shaft grip: Execute an upward shaft strike to lower ribs / downward crook strike (near horn) to head.

4. Pivot on balls of feet 45° CCW into HS: Execute horizontal shaft strike (chest high).

5. Pivot on balls of feet 45° CW to face B in RFS again: Execute high shaft block (both hands closed) / horizontal shaft strike (chest high).

6. Step forward into LFS: Execute lunge strike with tip end (both hands palm-down).

7. Right center kick to solar plexus toward B. While kicking, the cane is held as a guard diagonally across the front of the body with both hands, crook end high.

Toward C

8. Set right foot down from center kick toward D, pivoting body 90° CCW to face C in LFS: Release cane with right hand so it is now in the left hand as a mid-shaft grip. Execute left center block with downward pull to left side / straight upward strike with end of crook to face.

9. Step left foot back toward D into RBS facing C: As you are stepping, allow shaft to slide through hand into a reverse crook grip near the left hip with a right hand guard.

10. Step right foot back toward D into LBS facing C: Execute low swing strike to knees (left to right), ending on the right side where the right hand grips it palm-down in a mid-shaft grip.

11. Turn 180° CW by moving right foot to face D in RFS: Execute right center block with downward pull to right side / crook punch (to head, palm-down)

12. Step right foot back toward C into LBS facing D: As you are stepping, allow shaft to slide through hand into a reverse crook grip near the right hip with a left hand guard.

13. Step left foot back toward C into RBS facing D: Execute low swing strike to the knees (right to left), ending on the left side where the left hand grips it palm-down in a mid-shaft grip.

Toward A

14. Turn 270° CCW by moving left foot into LBS toward A: Execute left center block with downward pull to left side / crook punch (to head, palm down).

15. Step forward into RBS toward A: Bring crook end down so cane is level with the floor as a defensive guard / right hand grabs the grip, palm-down.

16. Step forward into LFS: Execute right center block, following through to rise up close to the right side, tip pointing toward A.

17. Step forward into RFS by moving right foot up to the left then out in a semi-circular motion: Execute a downward horn strike to the sternum (left hand guard) / Execute a #12 strike downward (from left side of body) so tip ends close to the floor. **[YELL]**

Toward B

18. Turn 180° CCW by moving left foot into LBS facing B: Bring shaft up and grip with left hand mid-shaft (palm up) as guard.

Step left foot back into standing posture, switch cane from right hand to left in a natural grip.

Repeat the mirror image of techniques 1 - 18 as follows:

Toward B

19A. Step forward into RFS: Execute reinforced center block (right to left).

19B. Switch to a double-shaft grip: Execute upward crook strike to the lower ribs / downward shaft strike (near tip) to head.

20. Pivot on balls of feet 45° CCW into HS: Execute horizontal shaft strike (chest high).

21A. Step forward into LFS: Execute reinforced outside block (left to right)

21B. Switch to a double-shaft grip: Execute upward shaft strike to lower ribs / downward crook strike (near horn) to head.

22. Pivot on balls of feet 45° CW into HS: Execute horizontal shaft strike (chest high).

23. Pivot on balls of feet 45° CCW to face B in LFS: Execute high shaft block (both hands closed) / horizontal shaft strike (chest high).

24. Step forward into a RFS: Execute lunge strike with tip end (both hands palm-down).

25. Left center kick to solar plexus toward B: While kicking, the cane is held as a guard diagonally across the front of the body with both hands, crook end high.

Toward D

26. Set left foot down from center kick toward C, pivoting body 90° CW to face D in RFS: Release cane with left hand so it is now in the right hand as a mid-shaft grip. Execute right center block with downward pull to right side / straight upward strike with end of crook to face.

27. Step right foot back toward C into LBS facing D: As you are stepping, allow shaft to slide through hand into a reverse crook grip near the right hip with a left hand guard.

28. Step left foot back toward C into RBS facing D: Execute low swing strike to knees (right to left), ending on left side where the left hand grips it palm-down in a mid-shaft grip.

Toward C

29. Turn 180° CCW by moving left foot to face C in LFS: Execute left center block with downward pull to left side / crook punch (to head, palm down)

30. Step left foot back toward D into RBS facing C: As you are stepping, allow shaft to slide through hand into a reverse crook grip near the left hip with a right hand guard.

31. Step right foot back toward D into LBS facing C: Execute low swing strike to the knees (left to right), ending on the right side where the right hand grips it palm-down in a mid-shaft grip.

Toward A

32. Turn 270° CW by moving right foot into a RBS toward A: Execute right center block with downward pull to right side / crook punch (to head, palm down)

33. Step forward into LBS toward A: Bring crook end down so cane is level with floor as a defensive guard / left hand grabs the shaft near the crook, palm-down.

34. Step forward into RFS: Execute left center block, following through to rise up close to the left side, tip pointing toward A.

35. Step forward into LFS by moving left foot up to the right then out in a semi-circular motion: Execute a downward horn strike to the sternum (right hand guard) / Execute a #12 strike downward (from right side of body) so tip ends close to the floor. **[YELL]**

Toward B

36. Turn 180° CW by moving right foot into RBS facing B: Bring shaft up and grip with right hand mid-shaft (palm-up) as guard.

Step right foot back into standing posture and switch cane to the right hand in a chambered crook grip.

Ready Stance (Chumbi)

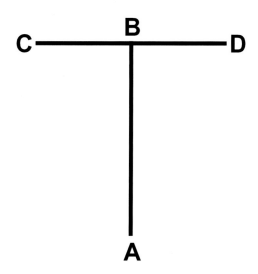

REFLECTION 5

Standing at A

Ready Stance (Chumbi) / Switch to natural grip.

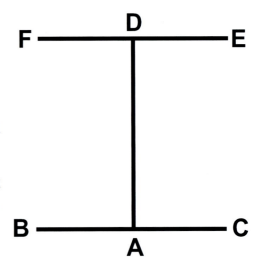

Toward B

1A. Step left foot into a LBS toward B: Execute left forearm block (tip up, double-shaft grip).

1B. Maintain LBS: Execute trapping technique (left wrist bends to bring left forearm to cane as it levels parallel to the floor in front of chest).

2. RFS toward B: Execute horizontal mid-shaft strike.

Toward C

Bring right foot to left and turn body 90° CCW so that your back is toward D in standing posture (eyes looking toward C). Lower cane to waist height, parallel with the floor. This is referred to as a transitional step.

3A. Step left foot out into LBS toward C (back is toward D): Execute left forearm block (tip up, double-shaft grip).

3B. Maintain LBS: Execute trapping technique (left wrist bends to bring left forearm to cane as it levels parallel to the floor in front of chest).

4. RFS toward C: Execute horizontal mid-shaft strike.

Bring right foot back to left: Stand facing C with back toward B. Lower the cane to waist height, parallel with the floor.

Toward D

5. Turn 90° CCW toward D into a LFS: Simultaneously, execute left knife hand block / vertical strike to the groin (as in CT-5, when cane is held in *right* hand).

6. RFS toward D: Complete the motion of CT-5 by turning right palm upward so the cane's tip points to the right, and thrust right arm forward at a slight downward angle. Maintain the cane parallel with the floor. Return the left hand as a fist to the chamber simultaneously.

244

7. Bring left foot forward and around to turn 180° CW into a RFS facing toward A: Execute a #12 strike downward from left side with the tip ending close to the floor. Left hand returns to guard position.

8. Step right foot backward toward D (body facing toward A) into a LFS: Execute a #11 groin strike upward toward D from right side looking over right shoulder.

9. Turn 180° CW by shifting right foot over into RFS toward D: Execute a #12 strike (from your left side) to the attacker's right clavicle.

10. Execute a left center kick to the solar plexus toward D. Set the left leg down toward D in a LFS.

Toward E

11. Pivot on balls of feet 90° CW into RFS toward E: Execute a center block. Project the shaft in front of you at a slight angle toward the left.

12. Step into LFS toward E: Execute a takedown technique (left hand grabs the shaft of the cane palm-down near the mid-shaft and pulls down sharply toward the left hip).

Toward F

13. Turn 180° CW into RFS toward F: Execute a center block. Project the shaft in front of you at a slight angle toward the left.

14. Step into LFS toward F: Execute a takedown technique (left hand grabs the shaft of the cane palm-down near the mid-shaft and pulls down sharply toward the left hip).

Toward A

15. Turn 270° CW into RBS facing A: Simultaneously, pull on cane shaft with left hand so right hand slides down into a crook grip, release the left hand, and execute a horizontal swing strike from left to right ending on the outside of the upper right arm (horn down).

16A. Step right foot back into LBS facing A: Chamber the cane under right arm (left hand guard).

16B. Maintain LBS: Execute a left knife hand block / Right reverse punch with crook down (left hand returns as fist to chamber) / left hand reaches up for a hair grab (right hand with cane returns to the chamber).

17. Execute right knee smash with left hand making contact downward onto top of right knee.

18A. Set right leg down toward A (as if bringing it behind attacker's legs) into a HS with body facing E/C side of kata: Execute takedown technique (right arm swings out and down toward left hip so the shaft under the arm presses into the attacker's neck).

18B. Maintain HS: Rotate right hand upward so palm faces to the left and the cane pivots in palm of hand so the tip now points toward the floor. Left hand grips upper shaft and right hand re-grips above left. Execute a strike with the tip of the cane straight downward toward the floor. **[YELL]**

19. Step left foot _behind_ right foot toward A into an X-stance: Slide left hand down to mid-shaft (palm-down), angling cane across the front of the body with crook end high (right palm up).

20. Step right foot out toward A into a HS: Execute a high strike with the end of the crook toward A (your right side) by driving with both hands in unison.

21. Move left foot to turn 180° CCW toward A into a HS (body facing B): Execute a tip strike to the back on your left side (strike directed toward C, right palm up, left palm down).

Toward B

22. Step into RFS toward B: Execute diagonal shaft strike with crook end high (right hand palm up) and tip end low (left hand palm-down).

23. Step left foot forward toward B and rotate your body 90° CW into a HS to face D: Execute takedown technique (tip end of cane raises up and then down in a lifting/throwing motion toward the right side).

Toward D

Bring left foot to right into a standing posture Facing D and tuck the cane under right arm. Left hand grabs shaft near crook, release the right hand, and lower the cane to the left side in a natural grip.

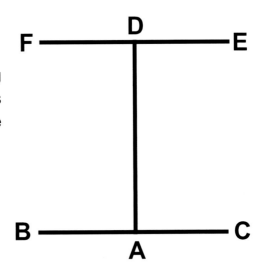

Repeat the mirror image of techniques 1 - 23 as follows:

Toward C

24A. Step right foot into RBS toward C: Execute right forearm block (tip up, double-shaft grip).

24B. Maintain RBS: Execute trapping technique (right wrist bends to bring right forearm to cane as it levels parallel to the floor in front of chest).

25. LFS toward C: Execute horizontal mid-shaft strike.

Toward B

Bring left foot to right and turn body 90° CW so that your back is toward D in standing posture (eyes looking toward B). Lower cane to waist height, parallel with floor. This is referred to as a transitional step.

26A. Step right foot out into a RBS toward B (back is toward D): Execute right forearm block (tip up, double-shaft grip).

26B. Maintain RBS: Execute trapping technique (right wrist bends to bring right forearm to cane as it levels parallel to the floor in front of chest).

27. LFS toward B: Execute horizontal mid-shaft strike.

Bring left foot back to right: Stand facing B with back toward C. Lower the cane to waist height, parallel with the floor.

Toward D

28. Turn 90° CW toward D into a RFS: Simultaneously, execute right knife hand block / vertical strike to the groin (as in CT-5, when cane is held in *left* hand).

29. LFS toward D: Complete the motion of CT-5 by turning left palm upward so the cane's tip points to the left, and thrust left arm forward at a slight downward angle. Maintain the cane parallel with the floor. Return the right hand as a fist to the chamber simultaneously.

30. Bring right foot forward and around to turn 180° CCW into a LFS facing toward A: Execute a #12 strike downward from right side with the tip ending close to the floor. Right hand returns to guard position.

31. Step left foot backward toward D (body facing toward A) into a RFS: Execute a #11 groin strike upward toward D from left side, looking over left shoulder.

32. Turn 180° CCW by shifting left foot over LFS toward D: Execute a #12 strike (from your right side) to the attacker's left clavicle.

33. Execute a right center kick to the solar plexus toward D. Set the right leg down toward D in a RFS.

Toward F

34. Pivot on balls of feet 90° CCW into LFS toward F: Execute a center block. Project the shaft in front of you at a slight angle toward the right.

35. Step into RFS toward F: Execute a takedown technique (right hand grabs the shaft of the cane palm-down near the mid-shaft and pulls down sharply toward the right hip).

Toward E

36. Turn CCW 180° into LFS toward E: Execute a center block. Project the shaft in front of you at a slight angle toward right.

37. Step into RFS toward E: Execute a takedown technique (right hand grabs the shaft of the cane palm-down near the mid-shaft and pulls down sharply toward the right hip).

Toward A

38. Turn 270° CCW into LBS facing A: Simultaneously, pull on cane shaft with right hand so left hand slides down into a crook grip, release the right hand, and execute a horizontal swing strike from right to left ending on the outside of the upper left arm (horn down).

39A. Step left foot back into RBS facing A: Chamber cane under left arm (right hand guard).

39B. Maintain RBS: Execute a right knife hand block / Left reverse punch with crook down (right hand returns as a fist to the chamber) / right hand reaches up for a hair grab (left hand with cane returns to chamber).

40. Execute left knee smash with right hand making contact downward onto top of the left knee.

41A. Set left leg down toward A (as if bringing it behind attacker's legs) into a HS with body facing F/B side of kata: Execute takedown technique (left arm swings out and down toward right hip so the shaft under the arm presses into attacker's neck).

41B. Maintain HS: Rotate left hand upward so palm faces to the right and the cane pivots in palm of hand so the tip now points toward the floor. Right hand grips upper shaft and left hand re-grips above right. Execute a strike with the tip of the cane straight downward toward the floor. **[YELL]**

42. Step right foot _behind_ left foot toward A into an X-stance: Slide right hand down to mid-shaft (palm-down), angling cane across the front of the body with crook end high (left palm up).

43. Step left foot out toward A into a HS: Execute a high strike with the end of the crook toward A (your left side) by driving with both hands in unison.

44. Move right foot to turn 180° CW toward A into a HS (body facing C): Execute a tip strike to the back on your right side (strike directed toward B, left palm up, right palm down).

Toward C

45. Step into LFS toward C: Execute diagonal shaft strike with crook end high (left hand palm up) and tip end low (right hand palm-down).

46. Step right foot forward toward C and rotate your body 90° CCW into a HS to face D: Execute takedown technique (tip end of cane raises up and then down in a lifting/throwing motion toward the left side).

Toward D

Bring right foot to left to stand facing D and transfer cane to right hand, chambered under right arm.

Ready Stance (Chumbi)

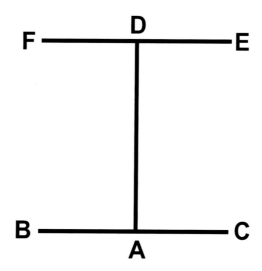

NATURAL WALK

You do not start and end this kata in the same location; rather, you move directly forward from your starting point at B toward A on completion. This kata does not have a pattern. The diagram indicates directions of movement for descriptive purposes.

Ready Stance (Chumbi) / Switch to natural grip

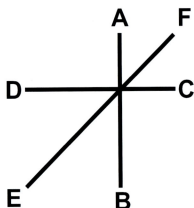

Toward A

1. Step back into RFS: Execute a vertical block, left to right (left hand grips the cane near the tip, both palms down / Block finishes over the right knee with the tip up).

2. Step back into LFS: Execute low shaft block (both hands closed on cane palm-down).

3. Step forward into RFS toward A: Execute a diagonal shaft strike to chest (the cane is held at 45° angle with crook end higher, both palms down).

4. Hook neck and execute left knee strike to solar plexus (switch right hand grip to palm-up, hook crook around attacker's neck from right to left, and pull cane to chamber on your left side near hip / Simultaneously, bring left knee up to attacker's solar plexus).

Toward B

5A. Set the left foot down in front of the right foot and pivot 180° CCW by bringing right foot around into LBS facing B. While turning, rotate the cane so that the left hand is palm up under right arm, the right hand is palm-up near the crook, and the crook is facing to the left.

5B. Maintain LBS facing B: Switch left hand to palm down, slide left hand up to crook and right hand back to end of shaft near tip. The left forearm is parallel with the floor. Push down sharply with the right hand to complete leverage technique. **[YELL]**

6. Facing B (backing up toward A), rotate cane crook upward and push shaft forward at a downward angle with right hand, allowing cane's shaft to slide through the left hand. Step left leg back toward A behind the right leg, then step right leg back into LBS. While backing up, rotate the cane and pull the shaft back so that your left hand slides down into a crook grip.

250

Toward C

7. Step left foot over 90° CCW into a LBS toward C: Execute a left high swing strike (cane shaft ends along upper left arm, right hand guard).

Toward D

8. Figure-8 techniques: Step left foot in front of right foot into an X-stance (moving toward D, body facing toward B): Execute 1½ figure-8's (½ from left to right, ½ from right to left, ½ from left to right, right hand guard).

Toward E

9A. Upon completing the figure-8 techniques, transfer the cane in flow from the left to the right hand and step right foot out 45° into a RBS toward E: Execute two additional figure-8's with the right hand (the shaft ends along the outside of the upper right arm, left hand guard).

9B. Maintain RBS toward E, but rotate upper body to face toward B: Execute right high swing strike from right to left, followed by right low swing strike from left to right (left hand guard).

Toward C

10. Bring left foot to the right foot, then slide left foot back out toward C into LBS. Bring the cane's shaft into the left hand (palm-down). Execute a downward tip strike (as left foot slides out, drive cane tip toward floor at a downward angle toward C, allowing it to slide through left hand). Note: rotate right hand so horn points away from the body. **[YELL]**

Toward F

11. Step left foot back CCW toward E into a RBS facing F: Execute ½ of a figure-8 (right to left).

12. Step back CW toward E into a LBS facing F: Execute ½ of a figure-8 (left to right), followed by horn reversing technique. Immediately chamber cane under right arm (horn up, left hand guard).

13. Step back toward E into a RBS facing F: Execute a horizontal swing strike from right to left. Grab the cane near mid-shaft with the left hand (palm-down) on the left side, switch right hand grip from the crook to natural grip on the cane's shaft (palm-down).

14. Step forward toward F into a LFS: Execute a center block to the right side, shaft parallel with the floor (cane in right hand, left hand guard).

15. Step forward toward F into a RFS: Execute a #1 strike to attacker's knee (to right side, left hand guard).

16. Step forward toward F, turning 180° CW into a RFS facing E: Execute a #12 strike from left side (left hand guard) **[YELL]**

17. Step the right foot around CW 180° into a RFS toward F: Execute a vertical block toward right side (left hand grips the cane near the tip, both palms down and tip up).

18A. Step forward toward F into a LFS: Execute takedown technique (extend tip end upward to left and then pull down sharply toward the left hip).

18B. Maintain LFS: Execute lunge strike to solar plexus with crook end (both palms down) from left hip.

19A. Step forward toward F into a RFS: Execute downward strike (bring tip end of cane up and down onto attacker's collar bone with the right hand (crook end) near right hip, both palms down).

19B. Maintain RFS: Slide right hand down into crook grip. Execute a tip strike to solar plexus by driving with right hand and allowing the shaft to slide through left hand. Left hand contributes to forward striking motion. **[YELL]**

Toward E

20. Step right foot around 180° CW toward E into a RFS: execute a horizontal swing strike from left to right (left hand guard). Shaft ends along outside of the upper right arm.

Toward B

21. Step left foot toward B into a LFS: Execute a downward swing strike, following through to left side.

22. Continue the flow from previous move: Execute ½ figure-8 from left to right, and bring

the left foot to right foot into a standing position facing B. Chamber the cane under the right arm crook down (left hand guard).

23. Step back toward A into LBS facing B: Execute a left knife hand guard (no power).

Toward A

24. Step left foot around 180° CW to face A in a standing posture: Lower cane so tip rests on floor in a crook grip at right side.

Ready Stance: Chamber cane under right arm, Chumbi.

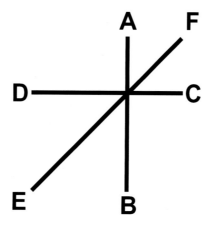

ANVIL

The following kata was designed in three segments, one from each of the founders.

This kata is the mental, physical and emotional challenge needed to bring together the many lessons of a journey well-traveled. Katas, also called forms, are the backbone of a style and demonstrate its history and its impact on the future. A first rank brown belt has reached the point where they have the moves and techniques required to do what is necessary. They have the flow and grace to be evasive and invisible in their movements. They have the mental awareness of right and wrong combined with the morality and virtue necessary to understand the importance of others and life itself. This kata allows the demonstration of all they have learned in a form that demands commitment, awareness, and responsibility for the actions taken. It requires you to see the attackers and understand what must be done, to emotionally yet calmly commit to these actions with the resolve to survive for those who need you and love you. To see these attackers for what they are, and the end result as a necessary conclusion, is to truly breathe life into this kata and seek peace and calmness by the completion of each action, which results in a personal awakening of yourself and who you have become, and how you can make a difference in the world around you each day.

This kata was designed to shape, form, harden, and sharpen, in effect to complete the process of making you, the student, a traditional black belt within your mind and heart, rather than the color of the belt you wear. May you embrace this form and the last part of your journey to black belt, making the school proud of you and you proud of whom you have become.

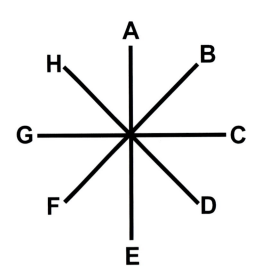

Ready Stance (Chumbi)

Toward A

1. Reach left hand across to grasp natural grip, step forward toward A into LFS and execute left down block directly from right chamber.

Toward H

2. Step right foot at an angle toward B into HS facing H. Execute a high shaft block followed by hooking technique to attacker's neck (extend the crook end of the cane forward while pulling the tip end back).

Toward C

3. Step right foot back CW toward E into a HS facing C and execute takedown technique (pull crook down toward right, shaft ends near your right hip). Execute a stomp with the right foot toward D. **[YELL]**

Toward G

4. Step left foot CCW into LFS toward G. Execute a lunge strike with the crook (left hand changes to palm up).

5. Step forward into RFS toward G. Execute #12 strike to the head with tip end of the shaft (left hand changes to palm down, right hand changes to palm up at mid grip) followed by takedown technique pulling tip end down toward the left (toward F).

Toward A

6. Draw right foot in towards left foot, then set back out into deep RBS toward A. Execute vertical strike to the groin (right hand palm up at mid grip, left hand palm down at grip). **[AUDIBLE EXHALE FROM UPPER CHEST]**

7. Step forward into LFS toward A and execute a strike to the face with the back of the crook (switch right hand to palm down, open left hand and palm cane so that the crook comes up in a circular motion directed toward the front, horn facing you).

8. Step forward into RFS toward A. Execute horizontal shaft strike. The horn will be facing slightly toward you for 8, 9, and 10.

9. Step forward into LFS toward A. Execute horizontal shaft strike.

10. Step forward into RFS toward A. Execute horizontal shaft strike.

Toward E

11. Turn 180° CCW by stepping left foot into LFS toward E. Release left hand and re-grasp the end grip below the right hand. Execute a low strike with the back of the crook from right to left (striking toward D).

Toward F

12. Step left foot into a LBS toward F: Execute a right low hooking strike from left to right (left hand releases the cane, horn faces towards right). Pull straight back with right hand toward right shoulder (pivot hips CW with this motion).

13. Re-grasp with the left hand at the grip, palm down. Perform a freeing motion by bringing crook of the cane up towards your left shoulder. Step right foot forward into a right leaning front stance towards F (bring right foot into left before stepping out): Execute a downward tip strike (left hand slides to a crook grip as you step, right hand grasps mid-shaft, and, tip strikes the floor to right side of right foot). **[YELL]**

Toward C

14A. Step the right foot CCW into RFS toward C: Execute a vertical block right to left, tip up (right hand switches to palm up, left hand palm down). This block is directed toward B.

14B. Execute head control technique by releasing the right hand, extending the right arm toward the right (palm away), and circling the right hand around to finish near your right hip (open hand palm up). These motions trap the attacker's head. Bring the shaft beside your arm near your hand parallel with the floor.

Toward C

15A. Bring left foot to right with body facing C. As you step up, bring right arm under the shaft so that the shaft rests in the crook of your right elbow. Continue to bring your right hand back towards the center of your body, palm facing away. Slide left hand to mid-grip. As you step up, bring the shaft up in unison near your upper chest height.

15B. Step right foot out toward D and drop into low HS facing B. This move results in a lower center of gravity, and the shaft drops in unison with this change with a slight drive downward with both arms on this motion. **[YELL]**

15C. Perform a releasing motion by bringing the cane shaft down and outward to the left with your left hand.

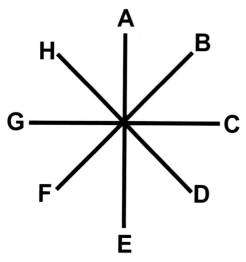

Toward A

16. Step right foot toward A into RFS (switch grip as you turn, right hand grasps above left at the grip, release left hand to guard): Execute right outside block, followed by a redirection/ trapping technique (continue the motion of the block so that the cane is vertical with the tip pointing downward toward the floor at your left side with horn facing to the left / Pull the crook end of the cane in a circular motion from left to right sharply down toward the right hip).

17. Step forward into LBS: Execute a left knife hand strike, following through with a takedown technique by rotating the left hand palm away and palming down to left side with the entire arm.

Toward E

18. Grasp end grip with left hand (palm down) and turn 180° CW into RFS toward E: Execute vertical block toward the right (tip up). Execute takedown technique by striking to the neck upward toward the left diagonally with the tip end, then bringing the tip end downward toward your left hip as you simultaneously pivot both feet and your body 90° CCW into LFS toward C.

Toward D

19. Pivot your feet and body 45° CW into HS facing D: Execute downward shaft block.

20. Pivot your feet and body 45° CW into RFS facing E: Execute left open hand high block toward D.

21. Pivot your feet and body 45° CCW into HS facing D: Execute right tip strike to the front. Left hand returns as a fist to chamber position.

Toward E

22. Pivot your feet and body 45° CCW into LFS toward C: Execute right reverse high block over your right shoulder (toward attacker coming from E, left hand guard).

23. Pivot your feet and body 90° CW into RFS toward E: Execute a #6 strike (left to right) to the attacker's head.

24. Step forward into a LBS toward E, grasp the shaft with the left hand just above the right hand palm down and thrust the tip forward, horn facing to the right (inserting shaft between attacker's left arm and body, crook catches wrist as you move in for next move).

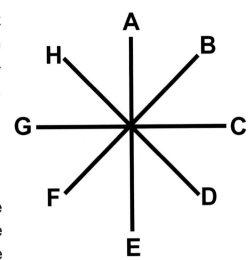

Toward C

25. Turn 90° CCW into LFS facing C by stepping the right leg around behind you. Simultaneously bring the cane tip up and around in a circular motion toward the left so that the cane ends parallel to the floor at the height of your waist.

Toward D

26A. Execute a horizontal rib strike with the shaft and follow through by pulling the right hand sharply across to the right hip and pivoting 45° CW toward D as the strike is completed and step into a RFS.

26B. Execute grip change by continuing to pull tip past attacker, bring the right hand (crook) up to your right shoulder with shaft resting to outside of your triceps tip down (your elbow will point straight ahead), and reach the left hand across your body to grasp the mid grip palm toward you. Release the right hand and execute a low hooking technique from right to left (horn facing left).

26C. Execute takedown technique by simultaneously performing a right long knife hand strike, pulling with your left hand toward the left, and pivoting on the balls of your feet CCW into left leaning front stance toward A, body facing C. Your arms will be spread wide to each side, and the crook will point toward the right in front of you (cane in left hand mid-shaft grip). **[YELL]**

Toward A

27A. Change right hand to crook grip (just above the horn), release left hand to guard. Shift left foot over into LFS facing A: Execute a groin strike to the front with the back of the crook (cane is vertical with tip close to floor, thrust right hand forward).

258

27B. Execute a strike to the chin with the back of the crook by raising your right hand directly upward (cane rises vertically, tip down).

27C. Execute a tip strike to the sternum (bring crook end down toward right shoulder to level the cane parallel to the floor, grab mid-shaft with left hand, palm down, and direct tip end forward).

Toward E

28. Right hand changes to natural grip. Turn 180° CW drawing right foot back into a right cat stance toward E: Execute a vertical block from left to right (tip up).

29. Right hand releases and re-grasps above the left hand, shift right foot into RFS toward E. Execute a strike to the face with the back of the crook.

Toward D

30. Release left hand to guard. Step left foot into LFS toward D, blocking across to the left with the cane held vertically, followed by a neck-hooking technique (rotate wrist so crook is directed toward the right, and strike from left to right). Simultaneously, execute left long knife hand strike and pull right hand toward right hip.

Toward H

31. Turn 180° CW drawing right foot back into a right cat stance toward H: holding cane in guard position with crook facing forward (right hand palm up, left hand palm down). The motion of the cane is close to the body with the crook passing by the left shoulder in a circular motion before the left hand grasps near the end-grip.

32. Step out into RFS toward H: Execute lunge strike with crook followed by an upward tip strike (maintain two-handed grip, bring tip end straight up and crook to left shoulder).

33. Step forward toward H into LFS. Execute hooking technique from left to right (maintain two-handed grip, extend right arm. Left hand will end palm up under your right arm, crook points toward right).

Toward D

34A. Turn 180° CW into LFS toward D by stepping the right leg around: Execute takedown technique by bringing crook end down toward your right.

34B. Execute a two-handed downward strike with shaft's tip end. **[YELL]**

This is done by bringing the crook upward toward your left (rotating right hand palm-up) while bringing the left hand and shaft to your left side. Continuing this motion by switching the right hand to palm down, releasing the left hand, and re-grasping below the right hand at grip with tip end raised (then complete the downward strike).

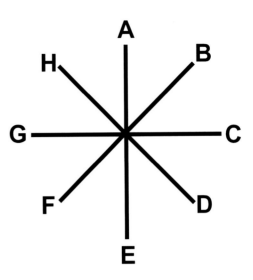

Toward B

35. Step into RFS toward B. Execute reverse high block with left hand supporting followed by #6 strike to the head (maintain previous two-handed grip for both moves).

Toward A

36. Turn CCW by dropping left foot back into RBS facing A. Execute ½ of a figure 8 (right to left, natural grip).

37. Step right foot back into LBS facing A. Execute ½ of a figure 8 (left to right, natural grip). Immediately chamber the cane (as the tip circles to the front, index finger opens and comes over the top of the cane. Allow the cane to continue its motion rolling over the other fingers and re-grab the cane in the horn-down position at the grip in the chamber).

38. Shift left foot over into LFS facing A. Execute right crook punch to the solar plexus. Grab with left hand, palm down above the right hand, and execute a low strike from right to left. Switch right hand to palm up and execute a vertical strike to the groin.

39. Step into RFS toward A. Execute takedown technique (thrust both hands forward maintaining shaft parallel to the floor, horn facing away) followed by downward strike with the tip end of the shaft (the cane circles around and down from the right side of the body). **[YELL]**

Ready Stance (bring right foot back to left, switch to right crook grip, Chumbi)

AUTUMN WIND

Ready Stance (Chumbi) at A, facing D, with cane chambered under right arm in a crook grip, then lower cane in front of you with left hand on top of right. Glance left, then right.

Swithch to a natural grip.

Toward B

1. Step back into RBS: Execute right center block (left hand guard).

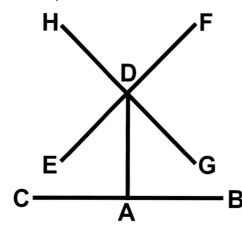

2. Skip-Step into another RBS: Execute a lunge strike (left hand grips the shaft just below the right, then right hand slides up to mid-shaft, palm up).

3. Pivot CCW on the balls of the feet into a left leaning front stance at an angle facing H: Simultaneously execute takedown technique by bringing the tip of the cane in an arc from right to left ending with the crook near left hip and the tip pointing downward.

Toward C

4. Shift left foot into LBS toward C: Execute left center block (right hand guard).

5. Skip-Step into another LBS: Execute a lunge strike (right hand grips the shaft just below the left, then left hand slides up to mid-shaft, palm-up).

6. Pivot CW on the balls of the feet into a right leaning front stance at an angle facing F: Simultaneously execute takedown technique by bringing the tip of the cane in an arc from left to right ending with the crook near right hip and the tip pointing downward.

Toward D

7. Raise left leg into a crane stance toward D (foot bladed): The cane is held vertically as a guard toward D (crook down, tip up) by releasing the right hand and re-grabbing the cane near the tip end of the shaft (palm away). Left hand holds the cane mid-shaft and the right hand is slightly above your head, over the left shoulder.

8A. Jump forward into left X-stance: Execute a low crook strike, then pull shaft toward right hip (by releasing left hand, jumping forward toward D, landing on the left leg with right leg crossed behind and on the ball of the foot. Swing cane around the head, and strike low from right to left, right palm up, then pull back). The knees are bent to lower the center of gravity, left hand guard.

8B. Maintain left X-stance: Execute a strike upward with the back of the crook (rotate the right hand so the horn points downward, left hand grabs the cane near the crook palm up).

9. Execute takedown technique (hook neck from left to right, continue motion by pivoting CW on the balls of the feet into a shallow RFS facing E). The horn points toward the right at knee height and the right hand (tip end) is near the right hip.

Toward E

10. Perform a crook-releasing motion. Switch the left hand grip near the crook to palm-down. Step right foot deeper into RFS: Execute left reinforced high block (right palm open).

11. Step forward into LFS: Execute left reinforced down block (right palm open).

12. Execute right center kick toward E, setting foot down into RFS. Cane is held with double shaft grip (palms down) in front of your body and parallel with the floor as a guard during the kick.

13. Execute left side kick toward E. Maintain the cane as a guard in front of you as in previous move.

Toward F

14. Set left foot down from previous kick into RBS facing F: Release left hand (right hand holds tip end of shaft) and perform a clearing motion by swinging cane straight out in front of you from left to right (horn leads). Continue to bring the cane CW around your body until the crook end of the shaft comes to rest against the back of left triceps. Right hand end behind your right lower back or hip area.

15A. Grasp crook of cane with left hand by reaching over the top, palm-away (this will be a reverse crook grip): Execute a figure-8 while taking two steps back into another RBS. Perform first ½ of figure-8 (left to right) while stepping right foot back to the left, and

15B. Execute second ½ of figure-8 (right to left) while stepping left foot back into RBS facing F. Immediately chamber cane under left arm, horn-up.

The next series of moves are done in flow toward F, but are presented here as six segments for descriptive purposes. 16. Segment 1: Step into LFS toward F: Execute a

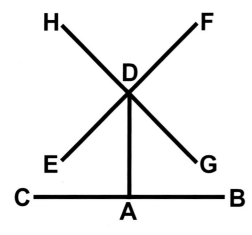

horizontal swing strike (left to right). As cane comes to your right side, switch hands by grasping crook with right hand (reverse crook grip in right chamber). Glance over the right shoulder.

17. Segment 2: Step into RFS toward F: Execute two overhead twirls into high swing strike. The overhead twirls are performed as the right foot comes up on the ball of the foot next to the left foot. The swing strike is executed as the RFS is completed. Following through from the swing strike, continue the motion by turning your body 180° CCW to face E (cane ends to your left side).

18. Segment 3: Step backward with left foot toward F (does not need to be a formal stance), facing E: Execute ½ figure-8 (left to right).

19. Segment 4: Step backward with right foot toward F (does not need to be a formal stance), facing E: Execute a figure-8 (right to left, left to right) that momentarily chambers at the right side (as you move into "step 5").

20. Segment 5: Turn 180° CCW while stepping with left foot into LFS toward F: begin two overhead twirls as you move into "step 6"

21. Segment 6: Step forward with the right foot into RFS: Execute a high swing strike toward F. **[YELL]**

Bring right foot back to the left into a standing posture: chamber the cane under the right arm with left hand guard. Glance over the right shoulder.

Toward E

22. Turn 180° CCW toward E by stepping right foot back into LBS: Execute left knife hand block.

23. Step forward into RFS: Execute groin hooking technique (performed by swinging crook forward from the chamber with arm extended), followed by left arc hand strike to the throat (right hand returns to chamber, cane horn-up). Glance left.

Toward G

24. Turn 90° CCW by stepping left foot back into RBS toward G: Execute low parry block (allow crook to rotate in right hand so tip points toward floor, left hand grips shaft below crook, right hand grips above left hand, block from right to left).

25. Step forward into LFS: Execute a vertical strike with the tip (perform this strike by first switching the left hand grip to a natural grip). Note: on completion of the strike, the left hand is near the left shoulder, tip pointing behind you.

26. Pivot on the balls of the feet CW into a right leaning front stance (body angled toward H, looking and striking toward G): Execute #11 strike upward.

27. Step right foot forward toward G into RFS: Execute a left reverse crook hook and right forearm smash to the face. Note: back of crook is held against left wrist/forearm with horn facing away and hooking left to right (tip points toward right). When completed, the left hand is near the right upper ribcage region, right hand is closed, palm-down with the elbow pointing to the front of the body.

28. Stepping back to standing posture facing G, 1½ figure-8's to chamber: From the previous position, grasp the crook with the right hand palm-down, step back with the right foot into LFS and perform a figure-8 (left to right, right to left), then bring the left foot back to the right in a standing posture and perform ½ figure-8 (left to right). Immediately chamber cane horn down under the right arm, left hand guard.

Toward H

29. Step back with right foot into LFS (body facing G): Execute a strike to the back toward H with the tip of the cane (cane on right side). Look over right shoulder and execute the strike with both hands on the crook of the cane.

30. Pivot on the balls of the feet CW (not a formal stance): Execute a downward horn strike to the shoulder toward H (left hand grasps mid shaft, right hand slides down to grip the shaft below the crook) then pivot CCW to face E as you pull the crook downward in front of you.

31. Facing E: Execute right axe kick. Note: hold cane horizontally in front of you waist high during kick.

32. Step back with the left foot into RBS facing H: Switch right hand to palm down and execute a right diagonal reinforced high block (left hand reinforcing and higher than the right hand).

33. Step forward into LFS toward H: Execute #5 horizontal strike to the head (right to left). Left hand returns to the chamber as a fist. **[YELL]**

Ready Stance: Bring left foot back to right to stand facing D, chamber cane at right side, Chumbi.

BRIAR PATCH

A

This form is executed with the use of a Bo-Cane or Walking Staff with a crook.

Facing A

Start by holding the bo-cane in your right hand palm forward with the tip on the floor and the shaft in front of your right arm with the crook forward.

Announce "Briar Patch Kata"

Bring the tip end up to your left hand (palm down) and grasp near the mid-shaft for a two-handed grip. The bo-cane is held diagonally across the front of your body with the space between your hands approximately shoulder width and the crook high to the right side facing forward.

B

Toward A

1. Step forward with right foot (walking step)

2. Step forward with left foot (walking step)

3. Step forward into RFS: Execute clearing technique from right to left with the crook. The shaft may slide through your right hand as the bo-cane is extended for the pull to the left side.

4A. Step forward into LFS: Execute clearing technique from left to right with the crook. This involves a hand change. As you step, the left hand releases and grasps the mid-shaft closer to the crook (palm-up) and the right hand remains closer to the tip (palm-down).

4B. Maintain LFS: Execute lunge strike with the crook to the solar plexus and retract the bo-cane.

4C. Maintain LFS: Extend bo-cane forward and downward hooking the lower leg with the crook facing left. Pull upward toward your right shoulder with both hands.

5A. Step forward into RFS: Switch the right hand to palm-up, and bring the tip end downward to the front. This is not a strike, but the motion is similar. Your eyes are directed downward at the attacker who is now lying on the ground.

5B. Maintain RFS: Look up to see next attacker coming. Execute tip lunge strike to the solar plexus (shift into a leaning front stance as you complete the strike). **[YELL]**

Toward B

The next series of moves involve four walking steps ending in a right cat stance. The lead foot will draw back and inward on the ball of the foot while the bo-cane completes its clearing sweep motion for each step. Once the bo-cane has passed the side of the leg, which is on the ball of the foot, that leg may continue to complete its step by moving out and backwards into the walking step.

6. Switch the right hand to palm-down about one-fist's distance below the left hand (both hands are now palm-down). Facing A, step right foot backwards toward B by bringing it near the left foot on the ball of the foot: Execute clearing sweep (on the right) into ½ of a figure-eight from right to left. As the shaft begins to turn over, switch the right hand back to palm-up. The hands will remain in this position for the remaining three walking steps and clearing sweeps.

7. Step back with the left foot into a walking step while completing a clearing sweep (on the left) into a ½ figure-eight.

8. Step right foot back into a walking step while completing a clearing sweep (on the right) into a ½ figure-eight.

9. Step the left foot back into a walking step while completing a clearing sweep (on the left) and begin to turn the bo-cane over to post it on the floor.

10A. Slide the right foot back into a cat stance, bringing the tip of the bo-cane to the floor (posting) in the center of your body. Your right hand will be rotated so the thumb is downward. Switch the right hand grip to palm-away and release the left hand, extending the left arm to the front with an open palm.

10B. Holding left open hand, look to the back toward your left turning the body and hips slightly and brining your left extended arm around toward B, then bring it back around to the front in the same manner.

Toward A

11A. Turn horn to right. Step into a RFS: Execute shaft strike to chest (left hand palm-down on tip end, right hand palm up on crook end) with horn facing backward.

11B. Execute a sweep to lower legs with the back of crook from right to left (slide right hand down next to the left hand as you strike).

Toward B

12. Continue motion of the sweep CCW turning your body to face 180^0 toward B by pivoting on your left foot and stepping into a RFS. As you step into this stance, the sweep rises up into an overhear twirl performed from a two-handed grip at the end-grip. In this stance, the shaft passes in front of the body at head height, continuing into the next step.

13. Step into a LFS: Executing an overhead twirl (two-handed grip).

14A. Step into a RFS Executing an overhead twirl that ends at head height, level with the floor, extended in front of your body toward B with the horn down.

14B. Simultaneously, reverse the grips of both hands so that the right hand grasps the cane from below and the left hand palms the bo-cane palm down. This motion should keep the bo-cane level with the floor at shoulder height. Grasp the bo-cane with both hands.

14C. Pull bo-cane down to your right side toward A in rowing motion (horn-up) between attackers legs and pull up and forward (your body faces B).

Toward A

15. Step right leg back into RBS toward A: Execute downward strike (tip ending near floor). [YELL]

Toward B

16. Turn CCW 180^0, step into RFS: Execute high shaft block (blocking overhead weapons attack, both palms down, left hand on crook end) followed by a strike with shaft (tip end) to upper ribs.

17. Step into LFS: Execute a high strike (left to right) and high hooking technique (to neck)

18. Rotate body CW and pivot feet: Pull crook downward for takedown technique. Counter with low strike (tip end). This is a strike to the attacker's head, but they are on the ground. [YELL]

Toward A

19. Holding bo-cane horizontally with crook at left, step right foot back into Left Walking Step.

20. Step left foot back into a Right Walking Step.

21. Bring right foot back to left into a Ready Stance.

Valley

Stand at A

Chumbi.

Change grip to right reverse crook grip, chambered / alternatively, may start with this grip.

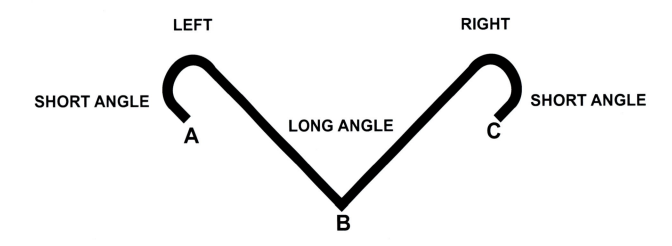

Toward Left Short Angle

1. Step into a LFS: execute an X-block with right arm on top (cane chambered horn up) followed by a left empty-hand center block *under tension* with right hand returning to the chamber.

2. Step into a RFS: execute a right center punch (cane horn up) followed by a left high palm heel strike.

Curving Toward Right

3. Step into a RBS (step left foot up to turn CW): execute a reverse brace block *under tension* (left hand grips mid-shaft).

4. Step into a LFS: execute a high strike (right hand slides down to left so both hands are grasping mid-shaft / crook posterior [away from attacker]).

Toward B: Left Long Angle

5. Step into a RBS: execute a vertical block (tip up) toward right side and lift up slightly (blocking right side kick and catching the leg).

6. Step into a Left Leaning FS: raise right hand over head (with crook) and left hand down, driving both hands forward to complete throw. Transition to the next move by bringing the cane around, in circular motion with flow (from the left).

7. Step into a Right Kihondachi: execute a vertical block (tip up) toward right *under tension.*

8. Step into a Left Kihondachi: execute a vertical block (crook up) toward left *under tension.*

9. Step into a Right Kihondachi: execute a vertical block (tip up) toward right *under tension.*

10. Step into a LFS: execute a left forearm strike upward to throat followed by a leverage technique and takedown (performed by raising right hand over head at an angle and then driving downward at an angle away from you with both hands).

11. Standing at B: Transition move: step right foot up to a Ready Stance facing the back. Rotate right hand palm up so the cane turns CW and re-grip into a natural grip with the left hand, releasing the right hand and re-gripping palm down near the tip end.

Toward C: Right Long Angle

12. Step into a LBS (left foot steps CW onto angle): execute a vertical block (tip up) toward left side and lift up slightly (blocking left side kick and catching the leg).

13. Step into a Right Leaning FS: raise left hand over head (with crook) and right hand down, driving both hands forward to complete throw. Transition to the next move by bringing the cane around, in circular motion with flow (from the right).

14. Step into a Left Kihondachi: execute a vertical block (tip up) toward left *under tension.*

15. Step into a Right Kihondachi: execute a vertical block (crook up) toward right *under tension.*

16. Step into a Left Kihondachi: execute a vertical block (tip up) toward left *under tension.*

17. Step into a RFS: execute a right forearm strike upward to throat followed by leverage technique and takedown (performed by raising left hand over head at an angle and then driving downward at an angle away from you with both hands).

269

Curving Toward Right

18. Transition: let the cane slide down through right hand into a reverse crook grip, and step into a RBS (step left foot up to turn CW): execute a reverse brace block under tension (left hand grips mid-shaft)

19. Step into a LFS: execute a high strike (right hand slides down so both hands are grasping mid-shaft / crook toward posterior [away from attacker]).

Right Short Angle

20. Transition: release the right hand, allow cane to slide into a reverse crook grip on left side of body, chamber the cane, and step into a RFS: execute an X-block with left arm on top (cane chambered horn up) followed by a right center block *under tension* with left hand returning to the chamber.

21. Step into a LFS: execute a left center punch (cane horn up) followed by a right high palm heel strike.   End at C.

Turn CW to face the front (bring right foot to left), transfer the cane to the right hand and chamber it: **CHUMBI**.

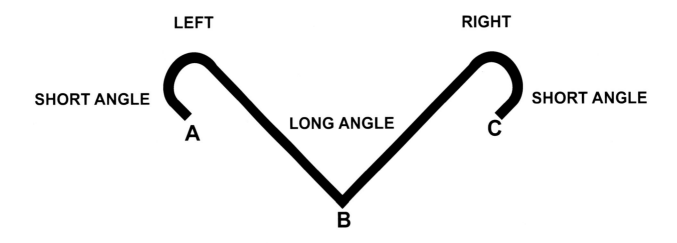

Old Man with a Cane

Old Man with a Cane was designed by Grandmaster Mark R. Shuey, Sr., the founder of Cane Masters International Association and the American Cane System Virtual Dojo. Grandmaster Shuey designed this kata as a tournament kata and won many competitions performing. He released three DVDs containing Old Man with a Cane, and while these forms have the same name, there are differences. They can be found on Black Belt Ranking Video (released for CMIA affiliates), Winning Katas and Advanced Techniques

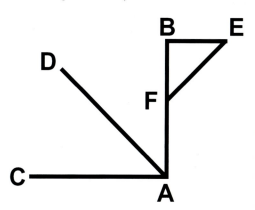

(for competition), and the American Cane System Level 8 DVD. The American Eagle Cane Style has come to do this form from Grandmaster Crandall's, Master Stalloch's, and Master Jessee's affiliation with Grandmaster Shuey as Senior Canemasters in his organization. The version of Old Man with a Cane kept alive and performed by American Eagle Cane Style is the traditional format of the form documented on the American Cane System Level 8 DVD.

This form does not have a rigid pattern; instead, it has directions that are faced while fighting off imaginary attackers. The diagram indicates these directions for the purpose of documentation.

Standing at A (Facing B)

Ready Stance (Chumbi)

Right hand on top of the crook, the tip of the cane on the ground, and the left hand on top of the right.

Facing Toward B:

1. Switch right hand to a natural grip, step right foot back into LBS facing B: execute a Center Block with left hand guard.

2. Skip-Step LBS: execute a Lunge Strike. Left hand grabs the cane mid-shaft, palm-up. As left foot begins skip-step, the cane is brought back toward the right hip. As the left foot sets down, the right foot slides up into the LBS, and the lunge strike is executed.

3. Skip-Step LBS: execute a Lunge Strike. Left hand grabs the cane mid-shaft, palm-up. As left foot begins skip-step, the cane is brought back toward the right hip. As the left foot sets down, the right foot slides up into the LBS, and the lunge strike is executed.

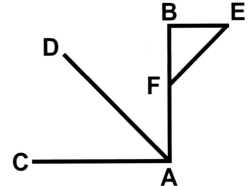

4. Step into RFS (change left hand grip to palm-down and re-grip right hand above left hand, palm-up): execute a High Crook Strike to the neck from right to left Pull shaft of the cane with left hand to left hip and slide right hand up to just below crook, and execute a left knee strike to the solar plexus.

5. Set left leg down toward B into a Diagonal Front Stance: execute throwing technique, driving the attacker away with the shaft (directed by left hand's push). **[YELL]**

Facing Toward B, Moving Backward Toward A:

6. Step left foot back into a Right Walking Step: release left hand and step left foot back, and execute a ½ figure-8 (left to right) allowing hand to slide onto crook for reverse crook grip (horn up).

7. Step right foot back into a Left Walking Step: execute a ½ figure-8 (right to left).

8. Step left foot back into a Right Walking Step: execute a ½ figure-8 (left to right).

9. Step right foot back into LFS: chamber under right arm (horn up), left hand guard.

Facing Toward C:

10. Look right. Look left. Step left foot CCW 90⁰ toward C into LFS: Swing cane over your head (right to left) to begin an overhead twirl. Continue flow into next technique.

11. Step forward into RFS: As you are stepping, execute two overhead twirls. As you complete step into RFS, execute High Horizontal Swing (right to left), following through to end at left hip where the left hand catches cane and grips it mid-shaft, palm-down.

Facing Toward A:

12. Turn 180⁰ CCW toward A into right-Crane Stance (with instep of left foot hooked behind the right leg and the left knee pointing toward A). The right foot pivots in place and the left foot is brought back to form the crane stance. The cane is along the left hip.

272

13. Step left foot forward toward A into LFS: execute a Low Horizontal Swing Strike (left to right). Left hand guard.

14. Step forward into RFS: As you are stepping, execute two overhead twirls. As you complete the step into the RFS, execute a High Horizontal Swing (right to left) **[YELL]**, following through to end at left hip (left hand catches cane and grips it mid-shaft, palm-down).

15. Step right foot back to left into Ready Position (Standing) toward A: ½ figure-8 (left to right) and chamber under right arm (horn-up). Left hand guard.

Facing Toward C:

16. Step right foot back into LFS toward C (body facing A): Look over right shoulder. Grasp crook with left hand (both hands are now on the crook), and execute a tip strike behind you toward C using both hands.

17. Pivot on the balls of the feet CW toward C: switch grip (left hand grasps end-grip and right hand grasps above left. Execute a High Crook Strike to neck (right to left). Execute throw by pulling cane downward toward A so the crook points toward the ground while pivoting back on the balls of the feet. Bring crook up and grasp grip with right hand near crook (palm down).

Facing Toward A:

18. Raise right knee high into stomp setting down into a Standing Position (facing along line D): Execute a low #2 strike (left to right) **[YELL]**.

Facing Toward D:

19. Step left foot into shallow LFS toward D (in this posture the stance's depth is approximately half the distance of a front stance): execute a Reinforced High Block.

20. Step left foot forward toward D into a LFS, switch left hand grip to mid-shaft, palm-up: execute a Lunge Strike to the sternum.

21. Step right foot into RFS, switching grip to left hand mid-shaft and right hand just above it: Downward Horn Strike.

22. Slide right hand to near crook. Then execute an Upward Shaft Strike in line with the center of your body by lifting left hand.

23. Left Center Kick moving forward into LFS. The cane is angled 45° across the front of the body as a guard (crook high to right).

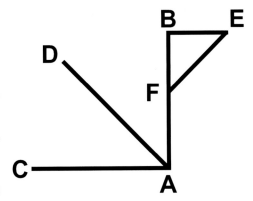

24. Right Side Kick toward D. As you execute the side kick, the right hand switches to palm-down and the cane is held hip height across the front of the body as a guard. Re-cock the kick without setting down. Hop toward D and pivot 180° to land facing toward A in a Crane Stance (landing on the right leg and hooking the left foot behind the right knee). As you set down into the Crane Stance, the cane is still held across the front of the body, hip height, and parallel with the floor.

Facing Toward A (Coming from D):

25. Set left foot down toward A into LFS: Reinforced Down Block.

26. Step into RFS: Switch left hand to palm-up, bring cane to right hip, and execute Two-Handed Crook Strike to groin (center of body).

27. Upward pull under tension into right foot stomp and downward strike with end of shaft (driving forward with left hand).

28. Step into LFS: Strike with shaft near tip to head (left to right) into strike with end of horn to head (right to left).

Facing Toward B (Coming from A):

29. Step right foot around and back CW toward B and slide left foot back into LBS: Reinforced Low Parry (left to right). The left hand reinforces the cane mid-shaft, palm-down. The cane circles up in front of the body; the cane comes from the left side as you turn (completing one full circle).

30. Sliding LBS: As you step, the left hand grabs the cane mid-shaft and it is brought back to the right hip. As you slide up to LBS, Lunge Strike to sternum, continuing flow into next technique.

31. RFS (then left foot slide up): Left hand changes grip to just below the right hand. Execute two-handed #12 strike (from overhead) as left foot slides up.

32. The left foot continues to slide up to the right foot, and the cane is brought down to the center of the body. Quickly step out into a RFS: Two-Handed Crook Strike upward to under the jaw.

33. Maintain RFS: bring cane down, switching right hand to grip palm-down near the tip (left hand palm-down near crook). Execute High Shaft Strike and recoil back to across front of body near hips, parallel to floor.

34. Left High Center Kick, re-cock kick and set down behind you, turning 180^0 CCW toward A into Horse Stance.

Toward A (Coming from B):

35. Maintain HS: Right hand releases cane. Down Block (right to left). Right hand guard.

36. Slide left foot over into LFS facing A: Bring cane up to right-side (crook down, horn toward you) and grab with right hand mid-shaft: Vertical Punch. Left hand chamber.

37. Right Center Kick moving forward toward A. As you kick the tip of the cane is pointed toward the floor and the cane slides through the palm (by gravity) until the tip rests on the floor and the right hand is on top of the crook. This is timed so the cane transition completes as you set the kick down.

38. Left Side Kick toward A, tip of the cane on the floor. Re-cock kick, turning 180^0 CW toward B, setting down and smoothly stepping right leg up into Crane Stance (right leg hooked behind left knee): Execute Down Block with left hand in chamber. Body faces C, knee faces C, technique done toward B. The hand slides down the shaft into a natural grip while beginning crane stance in preparation for the block.

Toward B (Coming from A):

39. Step right foot down toward B into RFS, bring cane to left side, and left hand grabs cane mid-shaft (right hand releases): Execute left Horizontal Punch (crook to left, horn to back).

40. Left Roundhouse Instep Kick (low then middle) and set down slightly forward toward B. As you set down, right hand grabs cane near tip and left hand releases.

41. Step right foot around 360^0 CW into a "crouching"-RFS (knees bent for sweep): Execute a low swing with crook end of cane (left to right). Continue flow of the cane upward near the right shoulder, grabbing with the left hand below the right. As you complete the swing through with the cane, straighten legs to rise up.

42. Step forward toward E into LFS: Execute a Two-Handed Low Crook Strike (right to left).

Facing Toward B, Moving Backward Toward A:

43. Slide right hand to a reverse crook grip by pulling on the cane's shaft with the left hand toward left hip, and release left hand. Step left foot back into Right Walking Step: Execute a side twirl into figure-8. The side twirl starts on the right side continuing into a figure-8 by turning the right palm-down. Execute the side twirl and 1st ½ figure-8 (right to left) as the left foot passes the right, and the 2nd ½ figure-8 (left to right) is completed as you start stepping back into the next Walking Step. *Continue flow into next technique.*

44. Step right foot back into Left Walking Step: Execute ½ figure-8, switch cane to left hand, and execute ½ figure-8. The 1st ½ figure-8 (right to left) is done with the right hand and it transfers the crook of the cane to the left hand. The 2nd ½ figure-8 (left to right) is executed with the left hand as you start stepping back into the next Walking Step. *Continue flow into the next technique.*

45. Step left foot back into Right Walking Step: Execute a figure-8. The 1st ½ figure-8 (right to left) is done with the left hand as the left foot is stepping back. The 2nd ½ figure-8 (left to right) transfers the crook to the right hand which completes the ½ figure-8 to the right side as the left foot finishes stepping back into Right Walking Step. *Continue flow into the next technique.*

46. Step right foot back into LFS: roll the cane over the back of the right hand on the right side as you step back and chamber cane under right arm as you complete the LFS (horn up). Left hand guard.

Toward D:

47. Step left foot over to left, into LFS toward D. Swing cane out from under arm and overhead. Step right foot toward D into RFS. Execute two overhead twirls while stepping, and execute High Horizontal Swing Strike (right to left) **[YELL]** as completing RFS. Cane ends at left hip where left hand grips crook and right hand releases into guard (reverse crook grip).

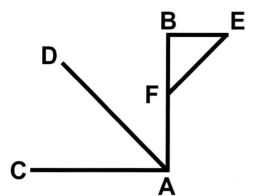

Toward E:

48. Step right foot over to right into RFS toward E. Step left foot toward E into LFS. Execute two overhead twirls while stepping, and execute High Horizontal Swing Strike (left to right) **[YELL]** ending at the right hip (right hand grabs mid-shaft, palm-down).

Toward F:

49. Jump off both feet and turn 180^0 CCW in the air, landing into Horse Stance looking toward F (crook facing F). Left hand re-grips just below the crook, palm-up while in the air.

50. Left foot skip-steps toward F into HS: Two-Handed High Strike with Crook (to face). As step begins, bring cane back to right hip. As foot sets down, execute the strike. As the back foot slides up, re-chamber the cane to the right hip. *Continue flow into the next technique.*

51. Left hand switches to palm-down, mid-shaft. Left skip-step into HS: Low Two-Handed Crook Strike (left to right), horn facing to front of body. Right foot slides up to left.

52. Raise left knee high, and execute a low left stomp forward, setting down to where the stomp was directed into a HS.

53. Raise the cane to the right side, releasing left hand and re-grabbing below right hand. Step into RFS toward F: Execute a Downward Two-Handed Crook Strike (horn facing down) **[YELL]**.

54. Bring right foot back to left into standing position: raising right and left arms to the side, palms facing forward (the cane is in the right hand, crook-up, and slides by gravity, down to a mid-shaft grip). Both arms lower to the sides. Eyes are directed downward.

Toward E:

55. Look over right shoulder. Left hand grabs cane (palm-down) near crook. Turn 90^0 CW, stepping right foot back toward E into Horse Stance: Execute High Lunge to sternum (both palms-down and hands above elbows) toward E.

56. Release left hand. Right High Crook Strike (right to left, palm-up). Hold this strike for the next technique.

57. Step left foot up to right. Low Right Side Kick / High Right Side Kick without setting down (Left Guard).

58. Set right foot down behind you at E (turning 45⁰ CCW) to face toward B into LBS. Execute cane releasing movement and lower the cane to front of body in a guard (left hand grips cane mid-shaft, palm-up).

Facing Toward B (Coming from E):

59. Maintain LBS, bring cane to right hip: Middle Two-Handed Crook Lunge toward B.

60. Step right foot into RFS toward B: Execute Two-Handed Downward Crook Strike to collar bone. As stepping, release left hand and grab near tip below right hand, and raise overhead. Hold strike in position for next technique.

61. Left High Center Kick. Re-cock kick. Set left foot down next to right foot. Turn 90⁰ CW to face B, stepping right foot out toward right in a wide step followed by left foot stepping toward right into standing position. While stepping to right: execute a sweeping takedown technique by pulling cane down low in front of body, releasing left hand and sweeping it up to the left side; at the same time, sweep right hand up to the right side (cane is in the right hand, crook up). Eyes are directed down.

Facing Toward B (Backing up toward A):

62. Raise eyes to front. Allow cane to slide down, by gravity, to reverse crook grip.

63. Step left foot back into Right Walking Step: ½ figure-8 (right to left). *Continue flow into next technique.*

64. Step right foot back into Left Walking Step: ½ figure-8 (left to right) as you start the step and, execute ½ figure-8 (right to left) switching to left hand as right foot finishes stepping into stance. *Continue flow into next technique.*

65. Step left foot back into Right Walking Step: ½ figure-8 (left to right), as stepping, into a ½ figure-8 (right to left) stepping, and ½ figure-8 (left to right) switching crook to right hand as finishing stance. *Continue flow into next technique.*

66. Step right foot back into standing position: ½ figure-8 (right to left), as stepping. ½ figure-8 (left to right) as finishing step into standing position. *Continue flow into final position.*

67. Step right foot out hip width and chamber cane (horn-up), fists slightly to front and sides of body.

Ready Stance (Chumbi)

278

INSTRUCTIONAL RESOURCES

BOOKS
DVDS
WEBSITES
SUPPLEMENTARY MATERIALS

Instructional Resources

The following books, DVDs, websites, and public service announcements are supplemental resources produced by the American Martial Arts Institute and its sister affiliate, Secure Living Online. All are available at Amazon.Com and more can be learned by visiting AMAI-EagleStyle. Com.

To Learn More Contact Us at 8382 Seneca Turnpike: New Hartford, NY 13413

(315) 768-1859

Books and DVDs

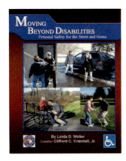

Moving Beyond Disabilities: Personal Safety for the Street and Home
By Master Linda Möller and coauthor Grandmaster Clifford Crandall, Jr.
ISBN: 9781463542436.

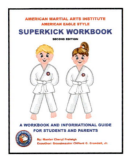

American Martial Arts Institute American Eagle Style Superkick Workbook
By Master Cheryl Freleigh and coauthor Grandmaster Clifford Crandall, Jr.
ISBN: 9781453727324.

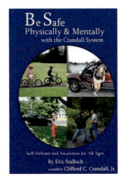

Be Safe Physically and Mentally with the Crandall System
By Master Eric Stalloch and coauthor Grandmaster Clifford Crandall, Jr.
ISBN: 9781449594695

The Tonfa: An Extension of the Mind and Body
By Grandmaster Clifford Crandall, Jr.
ISBN: 9780963660558

American Eagle Style Instructional Textbook

By Grandmaster Clifford Crandall, Jr.

ISBN: 9781478202530

Takenouchi-Hangan-Ryu-Matsuno-Crandall Iaido and Batto-do Textbook

By Kyoshi Nathan Morris and coauthor Headmaster Clifford Crandall, Jr.

ISBN: 9781449902568

Takenouchi-Hangan-Ryu-Matsuno-Crandall Iaido and Batto-do Instructional DVD

By Headmaster Clifford Crandall, Jr.

 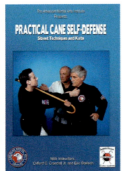

Cane-Fu: Moving Beyond Disabilities DVD

By Masters Eric Stalloch and Lynn Jessee, and Grandmaster Clifford Crandall, Jr.

Practical Cane Self-Defense, Volume 1 DVD

By Masters Eric Stalloch and Lynn Jessee, and Grandmaster Clifford Crandall, Jr.

American Eagle Style Self-Defense, Volume 1

By Master Nicholas Chuff and Grandmaster Clifford Crandall, Jr.

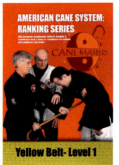

American Cane System: Ranking Series Levels 1-8

By Grandmaster Clifford Crandall, Jr., and Masters Eric Stalloch and Lynn Jessee (with support from Grandmaster Mark Shuey, Sr.)

Action Martial Arts International Hall of Fame Inducts Grandmaster Clifford C. Crandall, Jr.
Produced by the American Martial Arts Institute

Children's Self-Defense and Awareness, Volume 1 (3rd edition)
By Grandmaster Clifford Crandall, Jr.

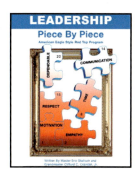

Leadership Piece by Piece
By Master Eric Stalloch and Grandmaster Clifford Crandall, Jr.
ISBN-13: 978-1500719487

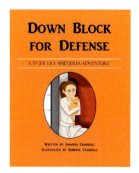

The Tiger Lily and Julia Adventure Series
By Amanda Crandall; Illustrated By: Sabrina Crandall; Editor: Grandmaster Clifford Crandall, Jr,
Down Block for Defense   ISBN-13: 978-1536958881
Center Kick for Confidence   ISBN-13: 978-1541307100
High Block for Hazards   ISBN-13: 978-1979049870

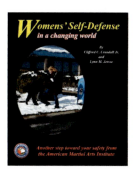

Women's Self-Defense in a Changing World
By Master Lynn Jessee and Grandmaster Clifford Crandall, Jr.
ISBN-13: 978-1796602340

Just Get Away: Secure Living Personal Safety Programs
Authored by Clifford C. Crandall Jr., Authored by Eric J. Stalloch
ISBN-13: 978-1495918728 (CreateSpace-Assigned)

Websites

AMAI-EagleStyle.Com   SecureLivingOnline.Com

TV

Martial Arts Today Show   Safety and Awareness Today Show Full episodes on our website.

Public Service Announcements

Visit AMAI-EagleStyle.Com to watch public service announcements produced by the American Martial Arts Institute and Secure Living Online. We have partnered with numerous agencies, including the McDonalds corporation to create PSAs for community safety.

Made in United States
Orlando, FL
11 November 2023

38832679R00164